HAUNTED KERNERSVILLE

D1521532

KELLY McGUIRE HARGETT AND SCOTT ICENHOWER

Haunted America

Published by Haunted America
A Division of The History Press
Charleston, SC
www.historypress.com

Copyright © 2021 by Kelly McGuire Hargett and Scott Icenhower
All rights reserved

First published 2021

Manufactured in the United States

ISBN 9781467147552

Library of Congress Control Number: 2021938373

Notice: The information in this book is true and complete to the best of our knowledge. It is offered without guarantee on the part of the authors or The History Press. The authors and The History Press disclaim all liability in connection with the use of this book.

All rights reserved. No part of this book may be reproduced or transmitted in any form whatsoever without prior written permission from the publisher except in the case of brief quotations embodied in critical articles and reviews.

DEDICATION

This book is dedicated to my father, John William McGuire. My father was born in 1945, which means he was absolutely a baby boomer. That alone shaped some aspects of his life. But there were so many other things that shaped him. He was born in South Carolina, and for a short while, he had a great childhood. His parents were not rich, in fact they struggled a lot, but they seemed to be in love with each other. My dad was the oldest of the three children, born in fairly quick succession. When he was just seven years old, his father died, leaving my grandmother alone with three very small children. She was unable to cope and left those three children. For several days, my father, a seven-year-old boy, took on the role of sole caregiver to his two younger sisters, ages five and three, somehow feeding them meals from what he could find in the kitchen, making sure they were clean and warm and most of all safe. A neighbor finally realized what had happened and was able to get in touch with my grandmother's family, and they came to get the children and rounded up my grandmother.

This began a long history of my dad taking care of the women in his life. My grandmother began a series of unfortunate relationships, during which my father took care of, and protected, his young sisters to the best of his abilities. My dad attended sixteen different elementary schools, if that gives you any idea of what his life was like. He even held himself back from going to high school so that he could stay in the same school with his sisters a little longer to ensure they were not picked on.

In high school, he showed a real athletic talent for football. He had hoped to attend a junior college on football scholarship, as there had been some interest from recruiters. The summer before his senior year, a guy from his high school thought it would be funny to pretend to hit my dad and three of his friends who were sitting on a bench in front of a local gas station. It may have been a funny prank if the guy's breaks would not have gone out. My dad almost lost his leg and the guy who was sitting beside him lost his life. There would be no football scholarship—there would not even be any football.

When my dad graduated from high school, the war in Vietnam was raging. My dad enlisted in the United States Marine Corps. During his basic training, while rappelling down a wall, he blew out his knee (in the same leg he almost lost in high school). He was honorably discharged from the marine corps, but once he was home, someone questioned his bravery. My dad, in his hardheaded way, immediately enlisted in the army. As a combat engineer, my dad served two tours of duty in Vietnam. He kept only enough from his paychecks to live on and sent the rest to his mother to take care of his sisters. I could write about the horrors he endured in Vietnam, but I will not. He did not like to talk about it, and in fact, he rarely did, unless I asked him specific questions.

Once he came home from Vietnam, he found a job and went to work. It would take a few years, but eventually, he met my mother, Glenda. They dated on and off during the summer of 1970. They dated "steady" for only a few weeks before they snuck off to get married. When I would ask my dad about this in later years, my dad would simply say, "When you know, you know." My parents had two daughters. We would often kid my dad about being surrounded by women his entire life—between his two sisters, wife, three sisters-in-law, two daughters and, eventually, five granddaughters, he was well and truly a man on an island of women. And he did what he had always done. He took care of us in the best way that he could. He provided a life for my sister and me that was more than he could have dreamed of as a kid. He started actually working a paying job when he was twelve years old just so that he could make sure his sisters got Christmas gifts that year. He never stopped working after that until he retired.

When I was a child, my dad worked a job that took him out of town, so when I was small, he seemed almost mythical to me. I remember he really liked to watch sports, Westerns and history shows on TV when he had "down" time at home. The sports and Westerns did not appeal to me as a child, but the history shows piqued my interest. I have always been a sucker for a good story, and if you know anything about history, you know the truth is usually stranger than fiction. The first historic thing I remember my dad talking to me about was the ships in the navy, specifically the *Monitor* and the *Merrimack*. If you don't know this story, it was the battle between the "ironclads" during the Civil War. It was also the first battle between ironclad warships. The names alone caught my interest. Later, I remember watching the old Disney show *Swamp Fox* with my dad while he explained to me that Francis Marion was a real-life person. It was those small moments that sparked my interest in history.

When I attended college and majored in history, I was able to ask my dad some real questions about his time in Vietnam. My dad shared information, along with some of his experiences, with me freely. My mother always said that he never talked with her about Vietnam, and as far as she knew, he did not talk with anyone else about it, at least not until much later in life when he joined a veterans' group. I think he shared information with me because he knew I was asking for academic purposes, not to judge him.

My dad and I were very close once I reached adulthood. We spent a good bit of time visiting with each other, talking about the state of the world—sometimes politics (although I tried to get out of those)—but mostly about cars, sports, history, his dogs and his granddaughters. When he died unexpectedly in summer of 2019, I felt my entire world shift. The touchstone of my life was gone. The last time I saw my dad was two weeks before he died. I was going on vacation the following week, so I came into town for several quick visits with family and friends that weekend. My oldest daughter was with me, and she had stepped into a mound of fire ants. As I tried to help her, I had gotten stung too. So, I did what all daughters do, I asked my dad for help. He was quick to find an ointment for us and help get us cleaned up and feeling more comfortable, and we were soon able to get on the road back home. He was always taking care of us—the women in his life. He never wanted it to be the other way around.

Although it was unexpected, I am still regretful that I could not get up at my dad's funeral and give him the eulogy he deserved. You see, he was one of my closest friends. Even as an adult, I still turned to him when I was unsure of which step to take next. He taught me valuable lessons like always sticking up for those who can't stick up for themselves and never making fun of someone for what they don't have. Those were the lessons life taught him at the sixteen different elementary schools he attended. He was always compelled to help those who may have been seen as weaker than those around them. To be honest, he had the reputation around my hometown of being a "fighter" in his younger days, and those fights generally came about because someone was picking on someone they shouldn't have. My dad would step in, and right or wrong, he would "correct" the situation. He most certainly was not perfect, and times were not always easy, but my father was a good and kind man down to his core, which was remarkable considering what life had handed him from the time he was seven years old. He would have never been called an optimist, but he was grateful for the life he had and the people surrounding him. He gifted me with an appreciation of the funny things in life, and he made me laugh with his quick wit and mischievous grin. He was my partner in crime at family gatherings, and we definitely shared a sense of humor and view of the world that others, sometimes, did not. He showed me that love was not selfish when he supported and encouraged me, even when I had hard decisions to make. In short, he was my dad, and I simply adored him. I just could not get up a few short days after losing him and find the words to explain to a room full of people who knew him what he had meant to me. I was too numb and too off kilter to get my thoughts in order. So, if you took the time to read the dedication in this book, thank you. Thank you for letting me tell you about my dad. He was one of a kind. There are so very many things that I miss about him, but I miss our conversations the most.

CONTENTS

CONTENTS

PREFACE

I never knew exactly what I wanted to be when I grew up. Like most children, my goals changed with whatever phase of life I was in. As a first generation college student, I didn't even really know what I wanted to major in. A friend's mother told me to major in communications, so I did. But as I dove headlong into my studies, I soon discovered that it was difficult to actually take any communication classes until I was farther along in my educational experience. I didn't want to waste my time in college, so I thought to myself, *I like history*, I'll just take a few history classes to fill my time until I can get into those communication studies classes. I quickly realized that I could double major and still graduate on time. And I realized, to my complete surprise, that I loved history. Nosey, sometimes to a fault, history let me dig deeper into the who, what and why of it all.

So, what is a girl to do who ends up with a degree in communication studies and a degree in history? Well, if she is lucky, she finds herself working for a local history museum where she gets to dig into the who, what and why of it all everyday. And if she is truly smiled on by fate, she ends up working in a little town named Kernersville. When my husband changed jobs so we could move back to our beloved home state of North Carolina, I could have never predicted when I pointed to Kernersville and said, "That looks like a cute little town, let's look for a house there," that I was going to fall head over heels in love with this place. But I did. I fell in love with the town and the people and their history.

And what a history it is! Kernersville, North Carolina, is located smack-dab in the heart of the Triad (Winston-Salem, Greensboro and High Point). It is a town with a rich and exciting history. And what I have learned as the director of the Kernersville Museum is that people love this town. Sometimes they are born here, and sometimes they move here. They put their roots down, they raise their babies here and they get involved in making the community a better place. And as I hope you will soon see, lots of them never leave.

One final comment: there will be plenty of you who will question if these stories are real. They are as real as any ghost story out there; as in, someone came to either my co-author, Scott, or myself and told us these stories. Names and occupations have been changed to protect the anonimity of those who shared their strange encounters and their hair-raising tales, but these stories are as real as the people who came in and shared them with us.

—Kelly McGuire Hargett,
executive director, Kernersville Museum

Acknowledgments

KELLY:

There are several people who deserve my eternal thanks for this project. Thank you to John Wolfe III and the Kernersville Museum Board of Directors for entrusting me to be the caretaker of Kernersville's history. It is a honor that I am extremly proud of, and I will always be thankful that you took a chance on me. Thank you to Jessica Bierman Gouge for teaching me everything I know and everything I don't know about museums, exhibit creation, artifact preservation and story presentation. Thank you to the Kernersville Historic Preservation Society for their support and their willingness to share information so freely. Thank you to the many citizens of Kernersville who have shared your stories with all of us at the museum, as well as those who have written stories and histories of Kernersville before me—your research and knack for storytelling is always inspiring. Thank you to Jerry Taylor, Janie Veach and Eddie Morphies for sharing your combined knowledge of Kernersville to help me draw clearer pictures of the town. And thank you to my dear friend Angela Jarman of Southwinds Gallery for always being my sounding board, no matter what.

I cannot thank my co-author, Scott Icenhower, and his wonderful wife, Katie Jo Icenhower, and the folks associated with Krossroads Playhouse enough for always being willing to jump in with both feet to my projects (hairbrained ideas) that sometimes seem to be more work for you guys than myself. ("Hey, you guys wanna do a ghost tour?" or "Hey, let's write a book.")

Thank you to my mother, Glenda McGuire, for always being my cheerleader; even us grown folks need that one person who still gets excited about our creations. You always encouraged me to read and write as a child. Thank you for helping me to fall in love with books and listening to my endless stories. And most importantly, thank you for reading to me as a kid, especially *Thomas, the Ship's Cat*. Freckles and I enjoyed it immensely.

And finally, thank you to my husband, Jason, and our beautiful daughters, Laney and Kayson Hargett. Your support and patience is more than I deserve. Thank you for being willing to eat so much takeout. Thank you for always being up for one more museum visit on family vacations just to appease my nerd heart. I love you guys more than you will ever know, and I am forever blessed that I get to be your wife and mom, respectively.

SCOTT:

Chronologically, I have to thank Molly Smith from the chamber of commerce for the suggestion of having a walking ghost tour of downtown Kernersville. Then appreciation goes to Kelly Hargett of the Kernersville Museum for letting me help with that. Then I have to thank Kelly again for realizing a book about Kernersville ghosts would be a good idea and allowing me to collaborate. Of course, I'm useless without my wife, Katie Jo. She was invaluable in all phases of this project. Thank you. Next are the town folk of Kernersville who were willing to share their stories of the supernatural. Thank you to The History Press for giving us a chance to share a little bit about our nightlife. And last but certainly not least, a big thank you to those spirits who stayed behind. I hope there are no critics in the afterlife.

INTRODUCTION

No good story is without a bit of mystery—maybe even a little bit of controversy. The story of Kernersville is no exception. We know that Native Americans traveled this area extensively. Although no tribes called this particular area home, it was a well-traveled trading route, which is evidenced by the artifacts that have been routinely found throughout the area over the years. Artifacts that can be traced to many different tribes let us know that they were traveling frequently through this area, trading with each other. When Europeans came and began to settle the area, large tracts were often purchased by newcomers to the area. According to noted historian, author, genealogist and translator Adelaide Fries, who was the foremost historian of Moravian history in the southern United States, the land that is today Kernersville was once purchased for four gallons of rum. According to oral tradition, sometime between 1756 and 1760, an Irishman named Caleb Story purchased four hundred acres of land some twelve miles east of Salem, close to the Guilford County line, and paid for said land with just four gallons of rum. There are others who would argue that this story is simply not true because there is no written record of this transaction. Where do we land on the controversy? We believe there is much value in oral histories, and if Adelaide Fries, who in our humble opinion was a giant among local historians, was willing to put it in her historical research, then there must have been merit to the story. But the truth of the matter is this: no one alive today was alive when the Irishman Caleb Story roamed this part of North Carolina. What we do know is this: the French and Indian War began in 1754 and ended with the treaty of Paris in 1763. During this time, rum was a popular commodity and was often used in trade. It was highly valued by the Native Americans. Many colonists found profitability in the alcohol trade, especially during this time period. During wartime, especially between the French and the English, trade would have been more difficult, making rum even more valuable than it normally was. So, the story of Caleb Story purchasing the four hundred acres that Kernersville sits on today for four gallons of rum right in the middle of the Seven Years' War makes sense to us.

No matter how the land was originally purchased, Colonel William Dobson acquired it around 1771. In the beginning, there was no planned town. This land was simply a crossroads, located on a well-traveled offshoot of the Great Wagon Road, and was the perfect place for an inn, Dobson surely thought to himself. Just as the crossroads had long been a popular thoroughfare for Native Americans, it was only natural that settlers would travel those same well-worn paths to trade themselves when they settled the area.

By 1791, the popular inn was used by President George Washington during his Southern Tour. According to his own journal, Washington visited the inn to eat breakfast after he left Salem and traveled to visit Guilford Courthouse battleground. Dobson would later sell the 400 acres, along with the inn, to Gottlieb Shober. In 1817, an ambitious man by the name of Joseph Kerner would purchase the inn, along with some 1,032 acres surrounding the area.

Joseph worked hard to develop the Crossroads into a real village. By the time his children inherited his property, Kerner's Crossroads was a thriving little village. Noteworthy events would take place here and there. During the Civil War, as schools across the country came to a stop, schools in Kernersville continued to operate. The railroad came through in 1873, in large part by the efforts of the citizens. From 1880 to 1888, the population of the town would double, going from just five hundred people to one thousand citizens. In 1938, Kernersville held a Fourth of July parade that attracted more than twenty-five thousand people. That is quite the feat for a town that had only around two thousand citizens at the time. It's no wonder that even today Kernersville can still draw huge crowds of more than thirty thousand people for its annual Spring Folly during the first weekend of May. We really know how to throw a party; it seems to be in the DNA here.

But what is it about Kernersville that draws people in? Could it be the location? Kernersville is some fifty to seventy-five feet higher than Winston-Salem. On clear days, you can see Pilot Mountain and the Sauratown

Sapp Hotel, formally Dobson's Tavern. *Kernersville Museum collection.*

Mountain range. It is located just twelve miles east of Winston-Salem and just eighteen miles from Greensboro. The land was described in an 1888 newspaper article as rich with "soil so well adapted to the growth of fine tobacco and grain, and fruits attain a rare perfection." Both of these features are points in Kernersville's favor, but we believe it's the hospitality of the people of Kernersville, which has been well documented through the years, as well as how much the folks who lived here really liked to have a good time, that draws people to this place. An article found in the November 17, 1888 edition of the *News and Farm* out of Kernersville, titled "Shadows of the Past: The Kernersville of Sixteen Years Ago," tells us what the Kernersville of 1872 was like. The writer of the article was Martin Holt, who attended school at the Kernersville Academy, and at the time he recounted his memories was the principal of Oak Ridge Institute, according to Mike Marshall and Jerry Taylor. In his memories, Holt recalled: "Kernersville when I knew it intimately had such an exuberance of social life, and such an unbounded, unstinted hospitality as is to be found only in towns remote from the great thoroughfares and commercial centers. Sixteen years have not effaced my memory of the hearty welcome which, from my entrance into the town and the school, made me feel I had friends indeed."

Square Dance on the Square, circa 1940s. *Kernersville Museum collection.*

Holt's description goes on to describe a wonderful Valentines party, the school picnics at Harmon's Mill, the epic picnics of Easter Monday, when the days were spent in "fishing, croquet, talking, walking, rowing and eating." Sounds like my kind of party. Clearly, Kernersville loved to party and welcomed newcomers with open arms and enfolded them among their ranks as though they were already family. Yes, it was a small village at this time, but Kernersville has never cared about how small it is. It was more about the size of the hearts of the people.

Although the town was officially incorporated in 1871, it continued to feel like a small village for many years. In 1921, the *Winston-Salem Journal* noted that, due to its location, Kernersville offered a "healthful climate, pure air and splendid surrounding country." This article also noted that "the people are cultured as evidenced by their splendid school system and churches." We know for sure that by 1922, Kernersville was shaking off the mantel of a small, outlying little community. The population in 1920 was more than 1,200 people, an increase of 10 percent from the 1910 census. This is particularly of note, since Kernersville was so close to a large city. According to the *Twin City Sentinel* in November 1922:

> *At present there are five miles of concrete sidewalk, and two miles more are being constructed. In all seven miles of concrete walks, which is more paved sidewalk than is found in many towns of this size in the state of North Carolina. Kernersville at this time is also putting in municipal water works and sewerage systems, an improvement seldom found in a town of this size. When all the now under way is completed, which will be within three months, Kernersville's populace will have all the conveniences found in large cities. Concrete sidewalks, water and sewerage systems, electric lights and modern fire protection. The people of the town are making Kernersville a most desirable place in which to live.*

So, it was this small village with a progressive attitude that would grow into a community of tightknit individuals by the 1940s and 1950s. This community nurtured its citizens as they in turn nurtured each other, as well as those who found themselves traveling through the town. It is a remarkable community, nestled in the heart of the Triad, that grew citizens who developed a deep love for Kernersville.

Fourth of July Parade, 1940s. *Kernersville Museum Collection.*

It is a community of people who care so much for each other, and their town, that they may never want to leave. So, join us on this adventure as we discover the history of this little crossroads community and the people who helped to shape it into what we see today. And as we uncover those who came before us, we will also come across those who have decided not to leave. Their reasons for staying are invariably their own and not for us to decide, but we hope you come to see that sometimes there are towns that are just too good to leave.

PART I

THE BELLAMY HOUSE

THE HISTORY

The 1870s brought change to the United States. Mark Twain had captured the essence of childhood with the publication of *The Adventures of Tom Sawyer* in 1876. The great American West was being settled, for better or worse. Small towns were growing rapidly, and that includes the little village of Kernersville. These were the changes that would form many towns into the vague shape of what we see today. Kernersville was officially incorporated in 1871 by the state of North Carolina, taking this place from a village into a town. The population in town limits rose from 147 in 1870 to over 500 after the railroad made its appearance in 1873. And it was in this fast-changing world that David Bodenhamer began courting Mollie W. Roberson.

In 1879, David and Mollie were married in Guilford County, North Carolina. The young couple were quick to set their sights on building a home near the crossroads in the little village of Kernersville. In 1880, work on the house that sits at 127 West Mountain Street was complete. Sitting within eyesight of the crossroads, the home was always a warm and welcoming sight. David and Mollie made the house a home for the next thirty years of their marriage and brought seven children into the world while they lived in the home. It was a lovely and warm home that was bustling with activity.

In 1915, the home was sold to Lizzie Sapp, a rather colorful woman in Kernersville's history. Lizzie was married twice but never lived with either

The Bellamy House, currently the Kernersville Museum. *Photo by Gina Childress.*

of her husbands for any length of time. In fact, her second husband's death certificate specifies that he did not live with his wife for the twenty years prior to his death. Lizzie owned several pieces of property in Kernersville, always listed in her name and not her husbands', but according to census records, she listed her occupation as a servant or domestic. At one point, she was also connected to a kidnapping in Kernersville. But Lizzie's story is for another day.

In 1919, George and Iona Bellamy purchased the home at 127 West Mountain Street. George worked for R.J. Reynolds in nearby Winston-Salem, while Iona was busy raising children. George and Iona had four children and raised them all in the home. It was a popular location for impromptu gatherings, with the rugs being rolled up, and dances breaking out in the living room. A pear tree grows in the front yard that is more than one hundred years old, and residents bragged about snagging fruit from it on their way to and from school each day without being caught by Mrs. Bellamy. The home remained in the Bellamy family until it was purchased by John Wolfe III and eventually donated to the town of Kernersville for the purposes of creating a local history museum, which was in 2013.

The Ghost Story

The first time the ghost made itself known was late in the afternoon on a Monday when the director of the museum was working in her office. On Mondays, the museum is closed, and the director uses this time to catch up on paperwork and accounting. As she sat at her desk, the hair on her neck stood up and she heard someone whistling the old tune "As Time Goes By" just beside her ear. Knowing she was alone, the director simply saved what she was working on, gathered her things and left for the day or forever. She was not sure at the time.

In the weeks that followed, the director found herself looking for items that she knew she just had. She eventually found that these missing items would reappear the next day sitting in the middle of her desk. And that is the thing about ghosts: if they can move things around, hide them and then bring them back, why can't they be more productive? Why not levitate a broom and sweep the hallway? They could whistle while they worked.

But let us dwell on this whistling phenomenon for a moment. During the summer of 2020, a local paranormal group named the Eclectic Paranormal Research Alliance investigated the Bellamy House. Using their equipment, the group captured the image of an entity hanging around the exhibits between a World War II uniform and an exhibit about Pinnix Drug Store. A psychic medium with the group explained that the ghosts in the Bellamy House are not malevolent but simply passing through.

That is our first clue. An entity drawn to a World War II uniform and just passing through? This boogie woogie boo boy probably has a girl in every spectral portal and was hitting on the director of the museum when he whistled in her ear. That is why he whistled a tune from a romantic movie from 1942. He could have whistled the "Colonel Bogy March" from *Bridge on the River Kwai*—that was during the war—or the theme song from the *Andy Griffith Show*, that's a lip purser, but no. Captain Apparition wanted to sweep her off her feet instead of sweeping the hallway.

The ghost took the hint and evidently was shipped out to the light. There has not been any whistling since. However, every now and again a few desk items will disappear only to turn up the next day on her desk. It seems like those ghosts who are just passing through cannot help themselves. It is a shame you cannot count them as visitors for grant applications.

THE P&N STORE

THE HISTORY

Part of the original tract of land Joseph Kerner purchased from the Schober family, this property, orignally located across the street from the tavern at the crossroads of what is now Main Street and West Mountain Street, has seen several different businesses. It is one of the most desirable locations to place a business, and William Henley purchased the property from Joseph Kerner's son Phillip when he purchased the inn at the crossroads in 1851. The property would pass hands and play host to millinaries and gocery stores. In 1907, Moses A. Stone purchased the property. Moses was a chewing gum salesman who had recently married Carrie Pinnix, daughter of a local reverand and schoolteacher, Joseph W. Pinnix. Carrie's brother, J.M. "Neighbor" Pinnix, would eventually acquire the property diagonally across the square from this property for his drugstore.

Carrie must have gone into her marriage with the high hopes of most brides. She was just nineteen years old when she married the thirty-one-year-old Moses A. Stone. We can imagine that Carrie had her entire life planned out. By the age of nineteen, Carrie had been working for four years as a schoolteacher, so marriage would have been the next logical step. However, things would not be easy for Carrie. She would spend the early years of her marriage traveling back and forth from Kernersville to Asheville, North Carolina, where her husband, Moses, was being treated for tuberculosis.

View of the P&N Store and Snow Building, circa 1930s. The wooden building just before the P&N store is thought to have been a millinery. *Kernersville Museum collection.*

They were blessed with one child, Mary, in 1910. We can imagine their joy at the birth of their daughter. But, their happiness was short-lived, as Moses sucumbed to his disease in 1912, leaving Carrie a young window with a two-year-old daughter.

Although she was widowed at a young age, Carrie must have had a head for business. By 1925, a brick building was contructed on her property on Main Street in Kernersville. The second floor of the building housed apartments available for rent, while the downstairs was home to a variety store operated by W.J. Johnson. By August 1940, H.C. Porter and E.T. Nash had purchased Johnson's stock and opened the popular P&N Department Store. The P&N served as one of the main department stores in Kernersville. It closed in the 1970s. The building was then available to rent by other businesses.

Carrie never remarried and always listed herself as Mrs. Carrie P. Stone. She passed away in 1972 and left the building to her child, Mary.

P&N Store decorated for the Fourth of July 1940. *Kernersville Museum collection.*

Her daughter sold the building in 1976. In 1980, local artist Richard Hedgecock purchased the building and opened his art gallery and framing studio. Rooms continue to be rented on the second floor of the building to this day.

THE GHOST STORY

Of course, rooms to rent means rooms to haunt. One of our newer residents, at the time of this writing, rented a room above the framing studio completely unaware of any such tales of apparitions among the partitions. While sitting in his living room with the door open to the hallway one evening, he caught a passerby in his peripheral vision. It took a few seconds to realize that the person walking down the hall had not made a sound. In fact, it did not seem like this person was even walking. It was more of a gliding motion. He listened for a moment and never heard a door open or close. This puzzle got the better of him, so he went to his door and peeked out into the hall. Then he saw her. She was gliding back toward him. He described her as a young woman, mid-twenties, wearing Victorian clothes. There was a mist around her that framed her body and replaced her legs from the knees down. That would explain why he never heard any footsteps—one would imagine. When he met her out in the hallway, she paused and hovered in front of him not making eye contact. He said her hair was pulled up in a bun-like hairstyle and the clothes looked expensive. She was attractive and had a thin waist thanks to a corset. What did she do in life that would cause her to be bound by a corset for eternity? Well, since she did not seem to have any lower limbs, maybe this was just an astral projection and she is in a better place with her hair down, corset off and eating chocolate. Either way, after a minute or so, the apparition vanished. Our newest tenant did not believe in spirits or partake of them either. So, as a nonbeliever, he was having some internal conflict.

Going back inside his apartment and closing the door this time, he wandered into his bedroom and claims he saw a little girl standing between his chair and small bedside table. She was dressed in clothes from the same time period as the lady in the hall. She also did not make eye contact. It was as if she was posing. He spoke to her, and she just faded away. Was that her mother looking for her in the hallway? Should he have left the door open? That usually is not necessary with ghosts. Still, he keeps it shut most of the time now. And now with a little ghost girl in his bedroom, where should he change clothes? At least she does not make eye contact.

Could this have been Mrs. Stone and her daughter or perhaps some tenants from long ago? Who knows? What we do know is that Kernersville has a new believer.

Charlie Snow's Diner

The History

In 1924, Charles F. Snow purchased the land and constructed the building that stands at 109 South Main Street. From one side of the building, Charles ran Snow's Department Store, where he had men's and boy's clothing. A barbershop operated on the other side. Ninety-six years later, a barbershop still operates in that same spot.

In 1947, Charles's son, Charlie, needed something to do. Unsure of what his future held, and surely feeling some pressure from his family to take a direction with his life, Charlie told his dad that he was going to build a roof over the alley between the Snow's building and the P&N Department Store, and he was going to start serving food. And he did. Charlie built a few walls and then a lunch counter and booths were installed, and soon, Charlie was serving up the best diner food around. Snow's became one of the most popular spots in town. Charlie operated his sandwich shop in a space that was just nine feet wide and seventy-two feet long. Looking at pictures of Charlie and his shop, you could not imagine a man more well suited to run a diner in the heart of Kernersville. From the pictures we have, Charlie does not look as though he was a very tall man, and in his later years, he wore dark-framed square glasses, a white short-sleeved button-down shirt and a black bow tie, his white apron tied around his waist. He looked like a character right out of central casting. Whenever a picture of Charlie is

Above: Charlie Snow standing inside his diner. *Kernersville Museum collection*.

Right: Fitz on Main, formerly Charlie Snow's Ice Cream Shoppe and Diner. *Photo by author*.

posted on social media by the museum, the comments come pouring in by locals who have fond memories of Charlie, the atmosphere he created in his diner and his impact on the town.

When Charlie Snow was operating his diner, each morning, local business folk found their way in for a cup of coffee and caught up on the news from town. Lunchtime was a crowded and busy affair, and then once school let out, in came the kids, with change in their pocket for an after-school soda or ice cream. Charlie knew everyone in town, and everyone knew Charlie. He operated the diner until 1985. After Charlie retired, a couple of different businesses tried their hand at making it work in the space, but it didn't work out until retired school principal David Fitzpatrick, who was raised in Kernersville and spent time in his youth going to Snow's, decided he would open a diner with the same small-town feel that Snow's offered years before. Fitz on Main now operates out of the same nine-foot-wide space that Charlie used all those years ago.

The Ghost Story

Fitz on Main, formerly called Snow's, continues the tradition of serving great food and being somewhat unique in that it just serves breakfast and lunch, closes at 1:30 p.m. and takes only cash. It has a fried baloney sandwich that is to die for. And speaking of dying, yes, it has a ghost.

Sitting in the diner to grab breakfast or lunch, if your attention gets focused on the staff as they work, you realize that it is almost like watching a well-orchestrated dance recital. They twist and turn, reach around one another, bow gracefully to allow each other to pass. It isn't an overt thing; it is all very subtle but still entertaining to watch. Working together for so long, they all seem to anticipate each other's moves. Rarely do we witness a collision among the quick-moving staff. The place opens at 7:00 a.m., but the cooks come in at 5:00 a.m. to start the day. Working in space that is literally only nine feet wide means that the staff are used to moving and working around each other. And every cook who has ever worked for Mr. Fitzpatrick has a story about feeling a tap on their shoulder or the brush of someone passing by when they are standing at the grill alone in the still, dark hours of the morning. One of the current cooks told us that while he has gotten used to getting a pat on the back every morning, he did not react as calmly when he watched his two spatulas move and cross each other while they were laying near the grill. It is one thing to think you feel a pat on the back. It is obviously quite another to watch your tools of the trade literally move before your eyes. Maybe someone wanted to pick up the old spatula and get to work for the day. It's possible that whoever is hanging around the joint does not realize that they are gone, and they are simply getting ready for the day. In any case, even when you get used to the strange happenings going on around you every day, it can still be unnerving to see the evidence move before your very eyes.

All we can figure is that even though Mr. Snow sold the property, he never really vacated the premises. He still likes to work behind the counter encouraging the cooks.

Snow's Building

The History

Charles F. Snow (yep, Charlie's dad) purchased the land at 113 North Main Street in January 1924. He quickly built the large, two-story brick building that still sits in that spot today. Charles constructed the building to open his own business, Snow's Mercantile. Ever the businessman, he had the building built so that he could rent space in it for another business, as well as space on the second floor. Since it was built, a barbershop or beauty salon has been located in the small front space in the building. Once Charles opened his mercantile, the local Masonic Lodge no. 669, which was chartered in 1931 and is still active today, used the space over his shop for its meetings.

After Charles F. Snow had closed his mercantile, and his son Charlie had built his sandwich shop next door (see Charlie Snow's Diner), the building did not sit empty for long. At one point, a Goodwill store took up shop in the space. At another point, it was a consignment shop. When Tiquer's Alley moved in, it offered different local venders a space to sell their goods. In short, the space has been used for many different kinds of businesses, but there is always a barbershop or beauty salon in the original front space.

Shops still come and go in this space today, and in a way, it pays tribute to the man who built the structure with the intention of offering usable business space to other entrepreneurs like himself.

Snow Building in the late 1920s. *Kernersville Museum collection.*

Please note, there was a Masonic Lodge located in Kernersville, Lodge no. 173, that began in 1855 and disbanded in 1873.

THE GHOST STORY

Houses are haunted. Cemeteries have spirits walking through them. But can an object be haunted? Maybe the energy or life force from someone is so intense that it remains after they have passed and resides in a picture, a mirror or a chair? And maybe you can find items imbued with the afterlife in an antique store.

Such was the case with the now-closed Tiquer's Alley that operated in the Snow building a few years back.

Bobbie Baker, who owned this store, told us that she bought a truckload of furniture and other items at an estate sale a while back. And among the things she bought was a rocking chair. She cleaned and dusted it and set it in a prominent place in her store. Over the next few weeks, she would notice the chair rocking from time to time. There was not a fan blowing it. Nothing had fallen on it. Sometimes she thought her husband or a customer might have sat in it to try it out, but when it started rocking by itself when she was in the store alone, well, that was a little unsettling.

She said one day a customer came into the store to look around. It was her only customer so far that morning. Bobbie greeted the customer; she replied in kind and continued shopping. After a few minutes, Bobbie heard the customer say, "Good morning, how are you?" Maybe this lady had some sort of short-term memory loss, and not to be rude, Bobbie greeted her again. "No, dear," the customer gently corrected, "I was speaking to the lady in the chair." The empty chair was rocking again. Bobbie was starting to look worried. "Oh, it's all right," the customer said. "I can sometimes see spirits, and there's a kind old lady rocking in that chair. She looks happy."

Could that have been the essence of the old lady's life force needing to sit down? You know the saying "you can't take it with you"? While that may be true, there doesn't seem to be any law stopping you from coming back to visit your stuff. Especially if it is a comfortable rocking chair.

Oh, just so you know, antique dealers are not required to tell you if any of the stuff they are selling is haunted, so buyer beware.

NORTH MAIN STREET

THE HISTORY

It is a block of buildings on North Main Street in Kernersville that grabs our attention next. These buildings were built behind what once was Dobson's Tavern and was eventually the inn the town's namesake, Joseph Kerner, would purchase. It would make sense that the land adjoining the inn would be quickly developed. This section of Main Street certainly has seen its share of business. Most people would be surprised to know that this block once housed Kernersville's first movie theater, called The Nymph, which was a silent theater. It was a dedicated place for moving picture shows, which was a point of pride for its citizens. There was also a nice millinery shop that Ms. Ranie Beeson ran for many years, offering the women of Kernersville fine clothing accessories.

Eventually, those buildings were torn down, and newer buildings were built in their place. The services offered out of those buildings often reflected the needs of a growing town. A dedicated post office was once located in these buildings. By the 1940s, Spiro Carello purchased a lot in the block and served pizza to his clientele. Next to him, Royal's Billiards opened, offering folks a place to grab a drink and play a game of pool. Today, the Street Boutique occupies the spot.

In 1926, John W. Corum purchased land on this block of North Main Street to operate his business, J.W. Corum & Son Plumbing. According to

Main Street, Looking North, Kernersville, N. C.

Above: Main Street, looking north, Kernersville, early 1900s. *Durwood Barbour Collection of North Carolina postcards, UNC–Chapel Hill archives.*

Left: View of the billiards room as seen from across the street. *Kernersville Museum collection.*

Top: Corum & Son Plumbing, E. Flynt, Grady Stockton, Oscar Corum pictured. *Kernersville Museum Foundation.*

Bottom: Block of buildings on North Main Street. *Photo by author.*

tax records, the building that now sits at 116 North Main Street was built by Mr. Corum in 1935. In 1938, Mr. Corum rented his space to a new business, Musten & Crutchfield, which would remain in the space until around 1941, when it moved farther up North Main Street, beside where it sits today.

Once Musten & Crutchfield left, it would not be long before the Shoe Center moved into the space. Gilbert Swaim opened his business and eventually took a wall out to expand his business into the next store over during the 1960s. The wall between the two stores is still open today, as the owners of each building have worked together to serve the merchants who have operated their businesses out of the joined spaces. The Shoe Center remained a staple of downtown Kernersville through the 1980s. After the Shoe Center went out of business, other businesses came and went from the space, including an exotic animal pet shop. Today, Pawlee's Doggy Bakery and Pet Market occupies the space.

And finally, next to Corum's building, at the end of the block, Dr. O.L. Joyner purchased a lot and built the building that still stands there today. He operated his dentistry office out of the upstairs. Dr. Joyner would become a prominent citizen in Kernersville, even serving as mayor.

The Ghost Story

As with all old buildings in downtown Kernersville, there are always tales of the mysterious bumps and groans. But it is the folks who work at the Doggy Bakery and Pet Market who have the most interesting stories. They say that before they open or just after they close, they sometimes hear the bell that is attached to the door ring. The door is locked, and no one is there. Soon after, they will catch a glimpse of an elderly man standing by the oven or the counter. When they try to look at him in full, he is not there. New employees have asked, "Who was that man who just walked by?" "Blue shirt?" the owners will ask for clarification. "Yeah," the employee will reply nervously, as they begin to realize that something is just not right. With a shake of the head, the owners reply, "That's our ghost." Apparently, he even triggers the motion detection cameras some nights, but his image has never been captured.

Because this location has been several businesses, everyone has their theories of who the ghost might be, but there is one more piece of evidence we must present.

When you walk in the store, the wall to your right is covered with individually wrapped dog chew toys hanging on hooks. Rubber bones, balls, stuffed animals, anything a dog would chew and could be made for their delight is hanging there. And they say that there have been several mornings when they open shop that all the tennis balls have been pulled down from the display wall. It is only the tennis balls, still in their packages, and the cardboard holes used for hanging them are ripped. Employees must repair the cardboard with tape before re-hanging them.

So, that could only mean that this elderly gentleman ghost has a ghost dog. Let us see—it is only the tennis balls, and they are at a certain height. Assuming ghost dogs do not levitate, it must be some sort of shepherd, sheepdog, collie, retriever type with an exuberant excitement for life—or death in this case. Anyway, it seems that the dog treat bakery is being terrorized by a kindly old shoe salesman and his haunted labradoodle.

Here is more evidence for a haunted Doggy Bakery. A local resident, who asked to remain anonymous, said that her dog Elle (the dog never said we could not use her name; our lawyers said we would be fine) will not go into that store. Elle must be carried into the Doggy Bakery. This is the only establishment this dog will not willingly enter. Furthermore, she looks for every opportunity to leave. Other dogs do not seem to sense any ghostly presence. This ghost just scares the Elle out of the place.

THE DAVIS HOTEL

THE HISTORY

The Davis Hotel sat on Main Street in downtown Kernersville. It's frustrating that no really good pictures of the Davis Hotel exist today. One picture gives us a glimpse of the porch from the street. A Sanborn Map from 1915 gives us a great idea of what the home looked like, but we must use our imagination to fill in the details. For those of you who might not know, the Sanborn Map Company created detailed maps of cities and towns in the nineteenth and twentieth centuries that were used by insurance companies to assess the liability of an area. From newspaper articles we know that the hotel was a twelve-room house that sat within eyesight of the train depot. The building boasted a large porch that wrapped around the house to one side. By 1909, newspapers boasted about Kernersville's ability to take good care of tourists and commercial salesmen, since it now had three well-equipped hotels in town. The Davis Hotel seemed to be the most "cozy" of the three, as articles of the day referred to "quantities of beautiful magnolias used as decoration, while in the parlor the same fragrant blossoms were placed on mantel, piano and table." Also, "renowned German artist Caesar Milch of New York City, who painted the frescoes in the home of Jules Korner, known as Korner's Folly, spent the holidays of 1912 at the Davis Hotel."

The Davis Hotel was known as a fine, family friendly establishment. Many people came and went from the hotel, on both short- and long-term stays.

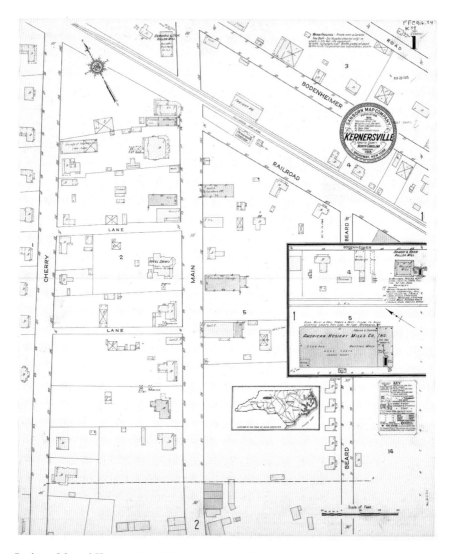

Sanborn Map of Kernersville, 1915. *North Carolina State Archives.*

Even some of Kernersville's long-term residents lived in the hotel for various reasons throughout their lives. Carrie Pinnix Stone and her husband, Moses, and daughter, Mary, were listed as residents of the hotel during the 1910 census. This was probably due to the fact that by 1910, Moses was suffering from tuberculosis, and he and Carrie were splitting their time between Kernersville and a sanatorium in Asheville, in the hopes of improving his health. The beautiful home had become a place of comfort for many in

The only known photo of the Davis Hotel. *Kernersville Bicentennial.*

Kernersville. So, it was a shock on the February morning in 1919 when the Davis Hotel was reduced to ash. The fire, it was believed, started near the roof of the building, from the kitchen chimney. Cinders and soot fell onto the shingles, causing the roof to catch fire. There was no shortage of help as people from all over town appeared quickly, ready to offer any assistance they could. But it was quickly apparent that the home was not to be saved. Citizens, as well as the Boy Scouts of Kernersville, worked tirelessly to keep the fire from spreading to nearby properties. In later accounts, the Boy Scouts would be praised for their tireless and energetic efforts to keep the blaze from engulfing more properties in town.

The property that the Davis Hotel sat on was eventually divided up among the Davis children. In 1950, the current building was completed. Originally, the building served as the home of the Kernersville Furniture Store, which operated out of the building for many years. Like so many buildings in Kernersville, the interior has undergone many renovations to accommodate new businesses. Today, the Kernersville Brewing Company has retrofitted the space to make it more modern and to fit their needs. Upstairs, Breathe Cocktail Lounge operates on the second floor. And next door, it shared a wall with the Eclectic Gift Shop. All three businesses were on the same lot that the Davis Hotel once occupied.

THE GHOST STORY

A poltergeist in a gift shop. That is what we have in the store named Eclectic, which shares a common wall with the Kernersville Brewing Company. Both of these businesses now sit in the block that the Davis Hotel once occupied. It was in that space that Eclectic inhabits that we are told of two shoppers walking among the antiques for sale who stopped to look at a hurricane lamp. You know the type (of lamp, not shopper). It has a base filled with oil. It uses a wick and has a large decorative globe that sits over the flame to defuse the light throughout a room. The lamp had been there a long time, but now, one of the shoppers was thinking about buying it. They checked the tag and thought the price reasonable but wanted to keep looking around. They were on the other side of the store when they heard an explosion and the sound of shattered glass. The hurricane lamp, while still sitting on the table, simply shattered.

Another incident involved an employee seeing a figurine fly off the shelf and smash into the opposite wall—not on the floor but the opposite wall. The owner of the store was not surprised. She had been sensing the presence of someone in the shop when she was alone. Once a friend told her she felt the presence of a young woman in the store who seemed to be filled with anger and emotion. Often employees have caught a glimpse of this ephemeral female's reflection in an antique mirror that was hung in their washroom. *Was* is the operative word in that last sentence.

No one knows who the ghost might be. There were no deaths recorded in the hotel—not even from the fire. A young woman did die by suicide, much later, in the McCuiston house located in the adjacent block. When that home was razed, perhaps she moved next door, forgetting the Davis Hotel was not there and ended up trapped in a gift shop next to a pub. That would make some people angry. And since ghosts can walk through walls, it is only a matter of time before we hear stories of beer mugs and wine glasses being broken.

BODENHAMER STORE

THE HISTORY

On January 27, 1889, Grover C. Bodenhamer was born to parents Jacob F. Bodenhamer and Emma J. Bodenhamer of Kernersville. We know that by 1910, Grover was listed as a laborer on the railroad and that he was still living with his father. In 1913, we found a Grover Bodenhamer listed as a waiter at the Star Café in Winston-Salem. This makes sense, in that on May 24, 1917, Grover C. Bodenhamer registered for the draft. The United States entered World War I on April 6, 1917. On his draft card, Grover stated that he was a "salad man" at the Clarke Hotel.

It did not take long for Grover's number to get pulled, and on September 18, 1917, Grover reported to his local board for military duty. He is listed as a private first class in the U.S. Army in the 321st Infantry (The Wildcats), Company D. We know that Grover is listed on the passenger list of the *Walmar Castle* on July 31, 1918, as he sailed off to war, where he arrived in France on August 16, 1918. He was released from the army on May 6, 1919.

According to the 1920 census, Grover now worked for his father as a salesman at the grocery store. Grover married Ida Angel in 1923, and just over a month after their wedding, Grover purchased a lot of land from his father on Armfield Street. In 1924, he purchased yet another lot, adjoining the first lot on Armfield Street. The 1930 census listed Grover as a salesman at the grocery store. In 1935, he purchased the property and the store on Main Street from his father. According to the 1940 census, Grover is listed as the proprietor of the grocery store, where he worked seventy hours per

Grover Bodenhamer's Store sometime in the 1940s. *Kernersville Museum collection.*

week. Looking closely at the picture of the grocery store from 1941, Grover offered gasoline, hot sandwiches, cold drinks, cigarettes and ice cream. Although the main level was used for a grocery store, the top level was used as a boardinghouse. The basement is the only one on North Main Street that still has the original coal chute. The chute would have been used when coal was delivered to the building for heat during the colder months. Although the building has been renovated over the years, the coal chute is still intact. Grover C. Bodenhamer died on December 1, 1979, at the age of ninety. We like to believe he was a wildcat until the end. The Bodenhamer family owned the property on Main Street until 1981. Today, H&R Block occupies the building that once housed Grover Bodenhamer's grocery store. What was once used as a boardinghouse upstairs has now been converted to apartments by the current owners.

THE HAUNTING

Grover Bodenhamer's store was fairly close to the railroad tracks that run through Kernersville. Kernersville had the reputation of being a rough and tumble town in the early 1900s. But by the time Grover was in business in 1935, the town was settling into the more idyllic small town most folks remember today. But that doesn't mean that everyone was always so peaceful. Grover used the second story of this store as a boardinghouse. Unlike the Davis Hotel that burned down years earlier, Grover's boardinghouse might not have always housed the more sophisticated set. After all, just down the street, even closer to the railroad tracks, sat Jinx Bull's establishment (which hosted pool tables and beer). So, the boardinghouse offered by Grover was in a great spot for those looking for a little mischief. As Grover was a World War II veteran, we would be hard pressed to believe that he just allowed any rowdy behavior, but Grover did not live in the building. It would not be a stretch to believe that some things might have gotten past him when his tenants were coming and going in the evening.

It seems as though some of those mischief seekers are still hanging around Grover's old boardinghouse. Although most ghostly happenings in the building today can be put into the category of "harmless," it is still unnerving to hear the bumps and thuds coming from the second story when there should be none. Is it the energy left over from the boardinghouse folks? The ones just passing through Kernersville, with no intention of making a home here but eager to enjoy the town's "hospitality"? The basement puts off an air of unwelcome and unease, causing most folks to avoid it at all costs. Surely, trudging down those steep steps late at night or early in the morning to shovel coal into the furnace was no fun and a task that no one wanted to do. A medium recently explained that unpleasant experiences often leave their energy in an area. Could the years of dread that went into trudging down into the basement leave the permanent uneasy feeling that the basement gives off? No one wants to get caught behind a door that has shut on its own, leaving them stuck in a creepy basement.

THE FURNITURE FACTORY

THE HISTORY

Tobacco was the lifeblood of North Carolina during the nineteenth and twentieth centuries; however, during the seventeenth and eighteenth centuries, North Carolina struggled with producing quality tobacco. This changed when a mistake was made during the curing process, and it was discovered that intense heat cured tobacco quickly, thus the birth of "brightleaf" tobacco. Around the same time, tobacco usage was changing from pipe tobacco to cigarette, which had become popular in Spain. As fate would have it, brightleaf tobacco was a perfect fit for cigarette production and became highly favored, as its cost was more affordable in America. Small factories began popping up all over North Carolina to meet the demands of this new product, and the economy soared.

Two brothers with a head for business, William H. Leak and James N. Leak of Guildford County, made their way to Kernersville in 1873 with the intention of building a tobacco factory. That building no longer stands, but at the time, it was the first of its kind in Kernersville and, as noted by George Winfree in the *People's News* in 1959, even before the R.J. Reynolds Tobacco Factory. Mr. Rynolds would later become a tobacco giant; however, he didn't build his first factory in Winston-Salem until 1875. The brothers would expand their business, and in 1884, they built the three-story brick building that is located on North Main Street and is part of what is now known as The Factory in Kernersville. According to local historians Mike Marshall and Jerry Taylor, the Leak brothers produced what was known as plug and twist tobacco and employed fifty to sixty workers. Some of their most popular brands of tobacco were Leak's Best and Cock of the Walk. The brothers had no way of knowing that in that same year, the Duke company would buy an exclusive domestic license to a machine that rolled cigarettes and drastically increased its output. By 1890, five tobacco firms controlled 90 percent of the American cigarette market. Although some small factories held on for a few years, this development effectively put an end to the small tobacco factories that had popped up in recent years.

However, the Leak brothers were nothing if not adaptive. By 1901, W.H. Leak had converted some of the three-story tobacco factory built in 1884 to the Victor Knitting Mill. Some of the building was simultaneously being used for a hotel as T.J. Willis operated Hotel Willis from the building from 1907 to 1910. This reinvention would become a hallmark of the building as it continued to be adapted and changed to meet the demands of the

The Factory buildings, on the left, is the original Leak and Company tobacco factory. The building to the right was a later addition, creating the complex we know today. *Kernersville Museum collection.*

The Factory as it stands today. *Photo by author.*

economy. By 1922, the Vance Knitting Mill had moved in the space once occupied by Victor Knitting Mill and was busy turning out ladies' hosiery. An additional building would be built beside the original to accommodate the growing Vance Knitting. Burlington Mills would occupy the space beginning in 1949, but by 1964, the building would see itself reimagined once again into a furniture-making factory when Lynwood Furniture Inc. purchased the space.

In 1972, the Hooker Furniture Company moved into the spaces, now including an additional building connecting the first two. For just over thirty years, Hooker Furniture manufactured furniture in downtown Kernersville. Residents fondly recall "smelling the wood from the furniture factory" throughout the town at all times of the day or night. For many people in Kernersville, Hooker Furniture kept their families fed and a roof over their heads. So, it was a blow to the community when, in 2003, the company made the decision to close the Kernersville facility, stating that it was the "oldest building and the smallest and the least flexible of all Hooker's plants."

The factory complex would not remain empty for long. Seeing the potential in the space, as so many people before them, today the complex is a mixed-use facility, with apartments in the upper floors, while the lower level houses various businesses and shops.

The Ghost Story

The Factory, as it is referred to today, has a lot of history, and apparently, you need history to have ghosts. One of the earlier tenants of The Factory, a hair salon, swears it has a ghost named Oliver. He has been around so long that current employees do not know if that was their name for him or if someone actually named Oliver, who, unlike Elvis, hasn't left the building. They say that toward the end of the day, the lights in different parts of the salon are turned off or on depending on what is more annoying. Oliver provides the requisite strange noises that a haunted salon should have. There are footsteps, creaks and the sound of things dropping to the ground. They never mentioned moaning and the sound of chains rattling, which is usually associated with less respectable businesses that we do not condone in our town. So, Oliver is a respectable ghost. However, he is a little mischievous. Hairbrushes, combs and other items move around or get lost. He is not a malevolent spirit—just a pain in the neck…or lower depending on who you are talking to.

Here is a second story. (The building has three stories. Not the same thing. This can be confusing.) The Factory is not a solid building taking up a city block. There is a courtyard in the middle of the place. It has a fountain and a small bridge. It is really a very beautiful and serene area. On several occasions, years ago, when the construction crew was building this courtyard, they would work late to stay on schedule. During those times, the men reported seeing a young lady running through the courtyard construction site wearing a white nightgown. They said she was very thin because they could see right through her. The history of this specter to date is unknown. Had she been a visitor to the hotel who Mr. Willis ran out of the space at one time? Perhaps she worked at one of the many factories that have been housed in those buildings and apparently overslept? Or is she the emanation of a tragedy that occurred on that ground long before any construction began? Unfortunately, it's a story we don't have the origins for, but we are intrigued, nonetheless.

One final tale to make your hair stand on end: In the not-so-distant past there was a wine shop on the ground floor of the factory complex, just beside the beautiful and serene courtyard. People would often go into the wine shop, purchase wine by the bottle or by the glass and then linger in the courtyard enjoying the surroundings as well as the wine. One spring evening, a few years back, two local ladies decided to check out the selection and enjoy some wine in the courtyard. As they sat talking, they realized they had begun to hear noises that sounded like large machinery turning on and then people talking and occasionally tools dropping. At first, they did not think much about this, but then it dawned on them, it was Saturday night. Not many people worked on Saturday night. Since there were shops in the factory, and some of the higher levels of the building were, and currently are, being converted into apartments, it was fairly easy to explore the factory buildings. They gathered their things and decided to go investigate for themselves. As they found themselves climbing steps and opening doors to see what was opened and what was not open, they got the eerie sensation of being watched. They soon found themselves as high as they could go in the space but still had not tracked down the source of the sounds, although they did find evidence of the construction of the conversion of the upstairs spaces into apartments. Just as they were about to give up, one of the ladies, let's call her "Stacy," caught a glimpse of someone. She turned to her friend and asked if she saw the man who had just walked by. Her friend hadn't seen him because she was busy looking out of one of the many windows. Stacy tugged on her friend's arm. She felt the distinct urge to follow this man. "Come on," she said, "let's ask him what we heard." Stacy told us later that she just knew he would be able to explain what they were hearing.

The two women took off down a long hall in the direction Stacy saw the man walk. Just as they turned a corner, she saw him up ahead, turning down another corner. Tugging her friend along with her, Stacy told us they were practically running to catch the man. By this point, Stacy's friend was put out with their journey. She stopped abruptly to catch her breath, pulling her hand out of Stacy's. When Stacy stopped, her friend told her she wasn't going to continue to run through the old building, as it was getting dark outside. It was beginning to feel creepy, and she was ready to go. Apparently, the courage the wine had initially given her was wearing off. Stacy reluctantly agreed with her friend but threw one last look over her shoulder. When she did, she swears that she saw the man they were following. He was standing at the end of the hall they were about to go down. He was wearing overalls, a '30s-style cap, and had an old red rag in his hand. He was peering back at Stacy and her friend while he was wiping his hands on the rag. When Stacy exclaimed to her friend, "Hey, look! There he is!" her friend looked at her like she had really lost her mind. Exasperated, she huffed, "There is no one there." Stacy looked back to where she had just seen the man. Her friend was right, there was no one there.

The two women made their way back to an elevator in the building. As they stepped in, they hit the button for the bottom floor. On the way down, the elevator stopped on the next floor down and another lady got into the elevator with them. Stacy took that moment to apologize to her friend for dragging her through the building and chasing the man in overalls. On hearing this, the lady who stepped into the elevator turned to Stacy and grinned. "Did you see Hank?" the woman asked her. Stacy looked at the woman confused. "Hank?" she asked. "Yeah, Hank." The woman laughed a little and went on, "He keeps a watch on the place. At least that is our theory. Was he wearing overalls and an old-fashioned cap?" Stacy nodded, growing paler by the second, according to her friend. "Yep, that's Hank. That's the name we have given him. Who knows what his real name was? My husband thinks he must have worked on the machines here when this was a knitting factory or maybe the furniture factory. Sometimes I just see him out of the corner of my eye, just as he is turning the corner down a hall. At first, he scared me, but now I just think, well, it's Hank."

This whole conversation took place on the rest of the ride down on the elevator and as the women walked their way back out to the courtyard. The woman patted Stacy on the arm and said sympathetically, "Dear, it was only a ghost. He can't hurt you. He was just continuing to do his job."

The courtyard at the Factory. *Photo by author.*

Stacy nodded in shock and looked at her friend, who was watching the whole conversation with wide-eyed interest. As the lady turned to leave the two friends in the courtyard, she looked back over her shoulder and asked, "By the way, did he have anything in his hands?" Stacy nodded, "Yes, a red rag."

The woman laughed, "That's Hank, all right." Then she looked up to the windows on the third floor that overlooked the courtyard and waved. The two friends followed her gaze up. There in the window stood a man in overalls and a cap. He raised his hand, in which he was holding a red rag, and waved.

Stacy and her friend gasped and clutched for each other. They turned to ask the lady if that was Hank, but she was gone, having already walked out of the courtyard. At least that was what they had hoped had happened. They hoped that they had not just rode an elevator and had an entire conversation with another ghost. No, Stacy said, she and her friend were at least 75 percent sure that the woman they were talking to was actually alive. But as for Hank, well, just be on the lookout for him the next time you are hanging out in the Factory complex and let us know if you see him.

The Grande Dame, aka the McCuiston House

The History

In 1896, Thomas Calvin McCuiston opened a bicycle service, repair and sale shop. He ran this business for several years, moving his shop around to different buildings. In 1903, he finally built a two-story brick structure near the railroad tracks and opened McCuiston Hardware Store, dedicating the rest of his life to hardware and similar businesses. From then on, he referred to himself as "Tom the Hardware Man." Hardware was definitely his specialty, but his store offered sewing machines, buck ranges (cooking stove), paint from Sherwin Williams and guns and ammunition of all kinds. He could fix just about anything. One of his specialties was making tobacco barn flues, which kept him working around the clock during peak tobacco season. By the 1920s, McCuiston's business drew people from neighboring towns. Tom was known to be honest and adhere to the policy of "honest square dealing with his friends and neighbors." He began adding "high grade furniture" in addition to his hardware offerings. His reasonable prices made his company a leading business in Kernersville. Later on, he bought the two-story building located across the street from his hardware store. The McCuiston's store would offer all classes of home furnishings, while he was also authorized to sell John Deere farm machinery. He really was able to offer just about anything the citizens of Kernersville could possibly want. His advertisements boasted, "We can supply you from your parlor to

McCuiston House in 1940s. *Kernersville Museum collection*.

McCuiston House in the 1960s, before it was torn down. *Kernersville Museum collection*.

your kitchen." Tom and his son, Kemp, operated a furniture store there for several years, and for many years, he was the only retail furniture agency in Kernersville. After Kemp passed away, Tom's youngest son, Phil, kept up that business for a while until he later opened a florist shop. The McCuiston family was in business for more than eighty years in Kernersville.

Thomas Calvin McCuiston was born in July 1872. In 1897, he married his sweetheart, Carrie Atkins. A picture in the *Kernersville Bicentennial* book highlights a picture of Tom and Carrie on a two-person bicycle with their first-born child, India, sitting in a basket on the front of their bike. After building his two-story hardware shop, Thomas built his wife one of the grandest homes in Kernersville in 1908. The home was described as "magnificent" and was two stories with four large columns supporting the main portico. The deep porch literally wrapped around most of the home in a semicircular fashion on one side. The home was the envy of many in Kernersville, with its stone base around the porch and walkway leading to the steps. Many folks recall heading to the hardware store with their parents just so that they could take their turn playing and running along the oversized grand porch. The large home would be needed because Thomas and Carrie had seven children. The McCuiston family would own the home until 1962, when it was torn down and the property was sold to the Musten and Crutchfield families.

The Ghost Story

By the mid-1950s, this once-beautiful house deteriorated into a dilapidated shell of what it once was. The dazzling white paint had faded and fallen fascia boards created the look of sad eyes as the boards fell over the windows. Signs of neglect on the outside told the tale of emptiness, abandonment and bleakness within. Houses of such grandeur, when they fall into disrepair, invariably take on the appearance of a haunted house to those who walk by. Such was the case with the McCuiston House.

The newspaper had an article headline that read "Search Is Ended." The search was for a young woman. Authorities dragged the lake and searched the nearby woods but couldn't find her. The rumor was that her parents forbade her from ever seeing the love of her life again. Someone that distraught would naturally gravitate to a place of emptiness, abandonment and bleakness. And so it was that the chief of police found the young woman's body in an upstairs room of the abandoned McCuiston House.

That day, the house fulfilled its destiny of being a haunted house. Because people who later would walk past the place and invariably glance up to look into the windows would have their morbid curiosity rewarded. They swore they could see her in the window looking down at them.

The newspaper stated that she took her own life with an overdose of barbiturates. However, a few of the town folk we interviewed said she hanged herself, and they claimed their parents saw that gruesome sight framed by the house's window on moonlit nights. Perhaps she manifested herself in whatever way people believed.

Either way, it's hard to imagine the grief and despair that could drive someone to take their own life, but sadly, it did happen there. And we're told that until the day the house was torn down, people, on occasion, would still see that desperate young woman in the window, and they were chilled to the bone.

The 1873 Depot

The History

The railroad in North Carolina changed the future of many small towns. In 1868, Forsyth County resolved that a railroad should be built from Winston and Salem (at this time they were still two separate cities, not the one city they are today) to connect to Greensboro. The citizens of Kernersville seized the opportunity and committed $10,000 to the effort. By today's standards, that project would be worth more than $26 million. That is a huge sum of money for a small village of people to come up with. By May 1868, surveys were being completed to begin work on the new railroad. Family records from the grandchildren of Joseph Kerner indicate that his grandson and namesake had been contracted to build a section of the railroad himself, along with thirty other men, by 1870. A letter to the editor of the *People's Press*, dated February 20, 1873, stated that residents of Kernersville had "seen the smoke and heard the whistle at the depot," indicating that their section of the track had finally been completed. The Historic Train Depot was completed that same year.

The depot itself was an impressive building for its time. Built on the north side of the tracks, according to the *Kernersville Bicentennial* book, "the single building included office, ticket window, passenger waiting room and freight warehouse." Piles of wood were kept near the building for the "firing of the train." The building was constructed with peg and mortice timber that can

The Depot as it looks today. *Photo by author.*

still be seen today. Also, the huge brick fireplaces that heated both the office and passenger waiting room can still be seen today and have been preserved for future generations to enjoy.

In something that would become a trend, it was reported in the *Western Sentinel* on February 28, 1889, that a reception room (what is assumed to be the lobby) was being added to the depot at Kernersville. The citizens of Winston expressed their desire for the railroad company to look after their needs in the same way, as "a similar room would be highly acceptable." Trains would soon run regularly from Greensboro to the Twin Cities, and Kernersville would reap the rewards of an economy that would soon begin to boom—a big accomplishment for a town that had only been incorporated two short years before. The railroad brought people and businesses to Kernersville.

SOUTHERN RAILWAY STATION, KERNERSVILLE, N. C.

Passenger Depot postcard. *North Carolina State Archives Digital Postcard Collection.*

In 1901, Kernersville was even blessed with a passenger depot that sat just opposite the freight depot. This was the source of some consternation for the citizens of Winston-Salem, which was much larger and no doubt more sophisticated than Kernersville. According to several articles in local papers, the citizens of Winston-Salem expressed their frustration and confusion that Kernersville would be awarded a passenger depot before they themselves had gotten one. One article in the *Union Republic*, dated October 31, 1901, was very tongue-in-cheek in its congratulations of Kernersville, stating, "While congratulating Kernersville on her good fortune, Winston-Salem trusts that the spirit of improvement on the part of Southern Railway management will continue to expand until the Twin-City is favored with passenger depot accommodations in keeping with the patronage our town extend and the merits of the case justify." The addition of the passenger depot was surely a feather in the caps of those who called Kernersville home.

The railroad brought all kinds of new things to Kernersville, including people, goods and even pets. The great orator William Jennings Bryan even included Kernersville on his popular whistle stops in 1906. One resident recalled his mother ordering a miniature pony from a catalogue and walking to the depot to pick up the soon-to-be beloved family pet. But the railroad did not always bring happy experiences. Trains obviously cannot stop quickly, and some citizens, unfortunately, would not survive their encounters with the trains that pushed progress through their town. Others would survive but be shaken up. In 1895, the *Union Republic* reported that a rock was thrown through the window of a train going through Kernersville. The rock missed a local district attorney named R.B. Glenn by half an inch. Although passengers were upset by the incident, the train did not stop. But we know that with growth comes growing pains. The railroad would shape Kernersville in many ways, and those ways can often still be felt.

THE GHOST STORY

The passenger depot was sadly torn down; however, this did galvanize the citizens of Kernersville to quickly work together to save the old freight depot that was built in 1873. The freight depot has been restored to its original state, with the addition of some modern conveniences, and it has been moved back a few feet from where it was first built.

A few years ago, this gentleman, we will call him "Sam" for the purposes of our story, was tasked with replacing some lightbulbs inside the old building. His coworker was outside checking and replacing lights outside the building. Sam was alone in the building and left to complete his tasks. He pulled out his tall ladder and climbed up to check the first bulb on his list. As he got to the top of the ladder and reached to unscrew the lightbulb, he heard someone cough and clear their throat. This startled Sam because he was sure he was alone in the building, and it sounded like it came from under the ladder he was standing on. Sam grumbled to his coworker that he should have let him know when he came in the building—he had startled him, and he could have fallen off the ladder. When Sam's coworker gave no reply, he looked down and realized he was still alone in the building. At that moment, a cool breeze blew across Sam's neck, and he had to force himself to stay still and calm and finish his task up on the ladder.

Once he was finished, Sam climbed down the ladder and walked outside the building to look for his coworker. He was working on the other side of the building, replacing lightbulbs there. Sam asked if he had come into the depot, and his coworker replied with an exasperated tone that no, he had not, he had been busy outside the building. Scratching his head, Sam went back inside the depot. He had three more lightbulbs that needed to be changed, and all three required him to climb his high ladder to do it. Each time he climbed the ladder and began changing out the bulbs, he heard the same coughing/clearing of the throat noise, always coming from just beneath his ladder. Each time he looked, he found himself alone in the building. Sam hurried through his tasks and let out a huge sigh of relief as he was getting ready to leave the building. Just as he was walking through the old lobby, getting ready to lock the building up, he heard a similarly exasperated sigh coming from the ticket office. Again, Sam felt the cool breeze on his neck (in a building with no air conditioning, in the South, in the summer). He quickly shut the door and locked it behind him, thankful that his tasks were behind him.

We wonder if it was the spirit of a former ticket agent who was following Sam around the depot that day. It is possible that he thought he was being helpful by holding the ladder for the maintenance worker. Maybe his sigh as Sam was leaving was in frustration that he had not been seen, or maybe it was in envy that Sam could leave and he could not. Either way, Sam told us that he tries not to go in the depot alone anymore, although he didn't really feel scared by the encounter, just a little intimidated by the thoughts of an unseen person watching him work.

But it isn't just the depot that holds onto the spirits of the past. The railroad itself was a blessing for the town, but at times, it was also a curse. For example, in 1878, a middle-age woman who lived near the rails ran in front of the train trying to shoo one of her pigs off the tracks. The pig survived, but unfortunately, she did not. Her dress was caught by the front end of the train, and she was dragged to her death.

In 1915, after an evening church service, a Mr. James Carter watched his children cross the track when a freight train was passing the depot. He panicked and chased after them. Blinded by the train's headlight, he lost his footing and was killed by the train. The children had made it across, but he could not see them.

At one point, a gentleman was standing on the caboose of the train when it was stopped briefly in Kernersville. Somehow, when the train started up again, this gentleman lost his footing on the back of the train; he fell off the back of the train, landing on his chest across the railroad crossties. The gentleman was placed back on the train and taken to the doctor in Greensboro, but his injuries proved fatal.

One of the most distressing stories is that of a widow named Mrs. Snider. The October 22, 1922 *Union Republic* newspaper stated that Mrs. Mattie Gray observed her mother, Mrs. Snider, walking along the railroad tracks just east of the depot. Mattie then saw the train approaching. She tried desperately to get her mother's attention, but it was of no use. Mattie watched the train run over her mother. The paper pointed out the whole train would have passed over her mother before it could have stopped. Poor Mattie was recently married and home to visit her mother and was sitting on the porch when the incident began to unfold.

This story lends some credence to the reports of hearing someone call frantically to their mother late at night, noting that it never sounds like a small child, but a grown person yelling for their mother. Some have even noted that on hearing the distressed calls, they will sometimes see a woman on the tracks, but she disappears as quickly as she is seen.

There have been stories of men who passed out on the tracks from too much alcohol and, well, you can imagine. In recent history, a young man was hit and killed by a passing train while he was walking on the tracks wearing headphones.

They say that in October, during a new moon, when there's a mist in the air, if you stand in the middle of the tracks long enough and face west, you will meet each and every ghost that is on this four-mile stretch of track. (That's because you will get hit by a train and become a ghost too. Our lawyers made us write that explanation so that no one gets hurt. Lawyers can be scarier than ghosts sometimes.)

Local Roots

The History

Alta Pinnix Smith lived in the home located at 247 North Cherry Street for fifty-two years. The house itself is nondescript. Built in 1928, it is a traditional craftsman bungalow–style home. But looks can be deceiving. The property was once owned by Alta's father, Reverend J.M. Pinnix. Reverend Pinnix had served in the Civil War. He and his wife had eight children. Reverend Pinnix was employed as a schoolteacher and a preacher and had acquired the land on North Cherry Street in the late 1800s. Alta was the youngest of those eight children. Her mother died when she was around two years old, and her father quickly remarried, possibly due to the number of children who were still living in the home.

The Pinnix children would go on to make their respective marks on Kernersville in different ways, all owning property and contributing to the growth of the town. Maybe because Alta was the baby and Reverend Pinnix had a soft spot for his youngest child, in his will, Reverend Pinnix specified his property not be sold until Alta was twenty-one years old, at which time the property could be sold and divided among his children. However, Reverend Pinnix died when young Alta was only nineteen. Alta's stepmother and siblings eventually deeded to her a portion of the land on the Pinnix Homeplace on North Cherry Street.

According to tax records, the home was listed in the name of Mrs. Alta Pinnix Smith. She had married Gilmer Smith, a World War I veteran. Alta

Local Roots, formerly the Alta Pinnix Smith home. *Photo by Katie Jo Icenhower.*

and Gilmer would have only one child, Kathryn, and through the years, census records indicated that they took on boarders in their home, possibly to supplement their income. Gilmer died in 1958, when Alta was just fifty-six years old. However, Alta lived in the home until she died. Alta left the home to her daughter, Kathryn, who sold the home in 1981. The home would switch hands four more times. Today, Local Roots Coffee Bar and General Store operates out of the old Alta Pinnix home on the land of the old Pinnix Family homestead.

THE GHOST STORY

We know that the Pinnix family owned a good bit of land around where Alta and Gilmer would build their home. And we also know from descendants in the family that Gilmer had quite a funny sense of humor.

Today, the owners and employees of Local Roots all say that they have heard strange noises from the attic and the basement. It is probably just the house settling. But what really gets them is getting locked behind some of the doors. Eventually, they get out of the back room or the restroom, but they cannot really explain what happens. They have replaced the doorknobs and reworked the door frames, but still, they can get locked behind some of those doors. They believe that mischievous ghosts, possibly the previous owners, are the key.

Although getting locked behind a door is understandably very unnerving, there are even more unnerving things that can be seen or felt outside the building. Years ago, teenagers would often get together in the evenings and roam around town to see what kind of trouble they could possibly get in. When it came to this particular section of North Cherry Street, they would slow their prowling. The house itself is very unassuming, but it is much bigger than one would think at first glance. One particular evening, two couples found themselves outside the home. The two boys decided to see who was the fastest. They would start side by side in front of the home, where they had each left their respective girlfriends. One boy would run to the right, the other to the left. The goal was to make it all the way around the house and back to the girlfriends, who would serve as the judge for who would win the race. One of the girls started the race with the typical, "On your mark, get set, GO!" The boys took off and, according to the girlfriends, disappeared around either side of the house. The girls stood alone on the sidewalk waiting, giggling a little nervously. They waited, and they waited. Five minutes ticked by, and the girls became convinced that the boys were pulling a prank on them. Just as they were deciding to walk together back to the car and wait for them there, one of the boys came running around the side of the house he disappeared from. He was sweating and out of breath. When the girls confronted him, the boy swore that he just ran around the house and that he was sure he had only been gone for a minute or so. As the girls protested, telling him that he had been gone much longer, the second boy came jogging around the other side of the house. Although he wasn't as sweaty, he was more shaken up. Both boys swore they never passed each other on their run around the house, but the second boy did say he stopped on the back side of the house. He said an older man came out of "nowhere" to yell at him for being disrespectful. When he tried to apologize, the man disappeared before his eyes. He stood there, shaking his head for a minute and then began to look for his friend, who he assumed would be by any second. He never saw his friend. He gave up and went to find the girls. All four kids (who are adults now) swear their tale is true. They did tell us that they hustled back to their car and decided to look for different means to entertainment from then on.

THE PEGG TEAHOUSE

THE HISTORY

The Pegg family can trace their roots in Kernersville back to at least the 1870s. According to census records, we know that Oliver found his way to Kernersville and was busy farming by the time of the 1870 census. Oliver and his wife, Laura, bought the property on Cherry Street in 1892. The home that sits on that property today was built by the couple in 1885.

Oliver would pass the home to his son, Junius (sometimes called James) Loton Pegg, in 1925. He and his wife would raise their family in the home. According to census records, Junius and his brother were both employed as photographers, and later, Junius was employed as a mail carrier. Whatever he did, he must have encouraged his son, Fred, to seek a higher education. Fred N. Pegg, who was born in 1901, became a dentist in Kernersville. Dr. Pegg and his wife, Fannie, would take over the home and raise their own four children in the home. The Pegg children were smart and active in the social scene in Kernersville. A search through old newspaper articles will yield multiple mentions of the Pegg children in various academic achievements and snippets from their social lives.

The home, noted for its Victorian architecture, was well loved by the Pegg family for more than one hundred years. It was not until 1991 that Dr. Pegg and Fannie's children would sell the home on Cherry Street. The Pegg house served as a Tea House for eighteen years. It was a place for brunch and

Pegg House as it looks today. *Photo by author.*

afternoon tea. As a social gathering place, it would have pleased the Pegg family. As of this writing, the house is currently the office and upstairs home to Walters Construction.

THE GHOST STORY

We are told that the Pegg family were very social people. Most weekends, they would invite friends over to play music with them in the parlor. Guitars were the instrument of choice.

Many a late night on the weekends, the young man who now lives upstairs claims to hear guitar music. Faint echoes of a good time had by friends who enjoyed each other's company. Present-day friends who visit Mr. Walters say they have heard the music too. A house where the good times never ended—now that is the way to be haunted. But it gets better.

The young man who lives there says that he is accustomed to the music, footsteps on the stairs and doors closing. He does not even get up to check anymore. He just says hello to the ghost and goes back to whatever he was doing. He and the ghost are just roommates now. And you know when you bring your girlfriend back to your place and your roommate's there, he will probably have something to say about her.

Whenever he brought his now-ex-girlfriend over, the noises and sounds around the house would increase and intensify. Once, when the young lady was in the downstairs bathroom, there were several loud knocks on the door and scratching sounds on the other side. He did not have any pets and he was upstairs. It scared her to death. If you are ever going to get it scared out of you, I guess that's the place to be.

In 2017, when all of this was happening, he took a picture of his then-girlfriend with his cell phone. When he looked at the picture, he said you could see the scowling face of an old man floating just behind the girl's head. It was unnerving to see a face just floating about her head. But on a lighter note, he did not think it was going to work out with her anyway, but it was nice to have a second opinion. The point is, ladies, he is single.

The knocks and bangs and scratching sounds inside the home would leave anyone a little shaken up, but for those who are simply minding their business, walking down the street, the sounds are truly a terrifying experience. Take for example the tale of one couple who were having an evening stroll, walking back from an early dinner on Main Street. As they came upon the Pegg House, the lady stopped in her tracks, claiming she heard a distinct knocking coming from the house. It got her attention because she thought the house was vacant. She tugged on her partner's hand, and they both said they felt pulled toward the house to investigate the sound. Taking a few tentative steps toward the home, the lady claimed a face of an angry man appeared in the window. She said he looked so angry that she instinctively stepped back. At the same time, her partner felt compelled to continue walking forward, almost like the house was calling to him to come in. Our friend was having none of that and pulled his hand until they were both back on the sidewalk. Once they were clear of the house and well on their way back to their own home, she asked him why he was trying to go toward the house. He claimed he heard soft music playing and just "felt" like he needed to go inside. What these two witnessed and felt is unknown. But what we do know is that they avoid the Pegg House on their walks to this day.

THE JOYNER, CRUTCHFIELD, MORRIS HOUSE

THE HISTORY

Oscar L. Joyner moved to Kernersville in 1914 and quickly began making a name for himself in the small town. A dentist by trade, Dr. Joyner was popular among the young social set of Kernersville. By 1917, young Dr. Joyner had met, courted and married Lucile Stafford, the daughter of local merchant W.C. Stafford. Dr. O.L. Joyner built the home at 109 South Cherry Street for his young wife, Lucile Stafford Joyner. The house has not always sat where it sits today. When it was originally built in 1919, the home sat on an adjoining lot facing West Mountain Street. While in the home, Dr. and Mrs. Joyner had five children. Dr. Joyner was elected alderman and served twenty-three consecutive terms during his lifetime and also served as mayor of Kernersville from 1936 to 1939.

We can assume that the young family outgrew the craftsman-style bungalow, because around 1940, Dr. Joyner sold his home on Cherry Street to Conard and Margaret Crutchfield. The Joyners moved to a much larger home farther up West Mountain Street, while the Crutchfield family settled into the well-loved home. At some point, before 1940, Dr. Joyner had the home moved to the lot where it sits today and turned around to face Cherry Street. A small service station was then built on the lot that the home had sat on. Conard and Margaret were happy and had two small daughters when they moved into the home around 1940. But happiness would not always be

The Joyner/Crutchfield/Morris house as it looks today. *Photo by author.*

the case for the young Crutchfield family. In 1949, tragedy struck the family when their thirteen-year-old daughter, Karen, died from a heart defect. Then, Conard passed away in 1962 at the age of fifty-one, in a car accident. Margaret would stay in the home until the late 1970s.

In 1980, Paul and Jane Morris purchased the home. For the Morris family, the home seemed to be a happy step in their long and joyful marriage. Their grandchildren recount many happy memories in the home. Sadly, Paul passed away in 2008 at the age of eighty-one, while Jane lived until 2013 and passed away at eighty-two. The family would eventually sell the home to the Town of Kernersville in 2017. The town then decided to allow the Kernersville Museum to use the property to expand its campus to have more room for the collections and education space.

THE GHOST STORY

During the summer of 2020, the Eclectic Paranormal Research Alliance, with the help of a psychic medium, investigated the home. A carpenter, electrician and painter would have been better, but you have to start somewhere.

During the investigation, the team discovered the presence of a middle-aged man who stayed in the front room of the home, near the windows that overlooked the gas station. It was possibly the presence of residual energy, and the team reported only that the "energy" seemed interested in looking out the window. Perhaps the entity could have been wondering where the gas station went because now there is a parking lot where the gas station once stood.

They also found the presence of a woman who walked around the home, dressed in her camel-colored dress coat and matching hat, adorned with a broach. Finally, the psychic picked up on the presence of a young boy sitting at the top of the steps. The boy was the only one who communicated with the medium during their investigation. He let the psychic know that he was just waiting on his brother because he usually babysat him. That was the only information he gave the psychic.

A combination of equipment like an EMF sensor and infrared thermometer coupled with the medium's gift allowed them to identify those entities and that confused "energy" looking out the window. The medium would also write down thoughts and or feelings that came to her while she was in the house. She usually kept those impressions to herself because they seemed random and could possibly be influenced by events outside the place she was investigating.

However, when the executive director of the museum was relating a story about the area behind the house and museum, the medium realized one of her impressions made sense after all. Three historical buildings had recently been placed back there to create a farm or village-like venue. Construction was almost complete but there were drainage problems. It seems the town planners had forgotten that the area had once been a fishing pond. It had been filled in over one hundred years before.

The medium opened her notebook and showed the executive director what she had written when she first entered the house. It read that a young boy had drowned out back. Some may scoff at the Alliance's other results, but that medium made a good first impression.

THE OLDEST BRICK BUILDING
IN KERNERSVILLE

THE HISTORY

In this block of buildings on South Main Street, opposite the Pinnix Drug Store building, sits the oldest brick structure in Kernersville. It was built in 1879 as a mercantile by John King, where he and his brother, Jim King, operated their storefront. Later, it was purchased by George Fulp and W.S. Linville, who operated a similar business out of the space. In the early 1930s, it was known as W&M Grocery, offering fresh meats and dry goods, located at what is now 104 South Main Street. By the 1940s, the popular Corder's Men's clothing store had moved into the space. In 1946, when the building next door was being built, Kernersville was moving from a sleepy, rural place to a more modern town. The need for more services was becoming apparent.

Just to the right of that building, Kernersville's first bank appeared on the corner of Main Street and West Mountain Street, at 102 South Main Street, in 1902. According to the *Union Republic*, in December 1909, Kernersville's bank was the strongest financial institution in Forsyth County outside of Winston-Salem. In an advertisement of the bank, we find that the bank opened a savings department on January 1, 1910, and "will receive amounts from $1.00 and up" with 4 percent interest compounded quarterly. The bank was often listed among the highlights of the town. A 1922 *Twin City Sentinel* article boasted that the bank had more than $500,000 in resources.

The Bank Building, early 1900s. *Kernersville Museum collection.*

Like many banks in 1933, the Bank of Kernersville was forced to close for a federally mandated bank holiday. But on reopening, the small bank brought in many new customers from neighboring areas because so many other banks failed to reopen. By 1951, the need for more space forced the bank to move across the street. In 1965, the Bank of Kernersville merged with Wachovia Bank and Trust. Throughout the years, the building has housed many different businesses, including Taylor Insurance Company, the Chamber of Commerce and a used bookstore.

To the left of the oldest brick building, 108 South Main Street was originally built in 1946 for Tri City Drug Store. Kernersville had officially grown from the need for only one pharmacy in downtown Kernersville (with Pinnix Drug "being on Square since 1904") to three pharmacies within eyeshot of one another. From banks able to stay open during the Great Depression to groceries, dry goods and clothing, this block of buildings was a "hub" of activity for Kernersville. This was surely a sign of Kernersville's growth and popularity. Over the years, many different businesses have occupied this block of buildings. So, it is no shock that we still hear tales of citizens who have long passed who are hanging around this particular area.

Corder's Clothing, circa 1940s. *Kernersville Museum collection.*

THE GHOST STORY

If everyone who passed did not pass but stayed, the oldest brick building in Kernersville would be overcrowded. Obviously, many souls have crossed over, but for those who didn't, should we try to understand them relative to the businesses they haunt and not just the building? For the following story, we have to wonder if those who are still lingering in our world could possibly get confused or maybe even curious about the newer businesses next door. Obviously, we cannot be sure.

The business in question was a wellness and nutrition store that rented the upstairs space at 108 South Main Street. It offered massage and nutritional consultations. Below, on the street level, was a private gym. The two were a good fit. Things were state of the art, and they had security cameras as part of their security systems. The reason the cameras are mentioned is that was how the ghosts were ultimately detected.

When items around the offices began to be continually misplaced and gym goers complained of feeling like they were being watched when they entered the changing rooms, the owner began watching the security footage from the previous nights. She saw orbs and floating lights darting about the place. The orbs would follow staff in and out of rooms and guests in and out of changing rooms.

These floating balls of light seemed to be responsible for exercise balls rolling across the floor in deliberate paths or hand weights falling out of their racks. However, the orbs would really pick up movement at night once everyone had gone home for the evening. Orbs gathering together could be seen moving in and out of rooms on the surveillance footage. If the security cameras did not provide enough evidence, a client scheduled for a massage who happened to be a medium told the owner that her building happened to have a lot of spirits hanging around.

Many ghosts can be recognized as people. Sometimes they are floating people without legs but still recognizable. Who are these ghosts? They are fat little balls of energy that ironically hang out at the gym. They do not work out and irritate those who do. There are a lot of people like that now. Perhaps some people never change.

Pinnix Drug

The History

"A busy businessman who was never too busy to be a good neighbor." This was the way John Marshall Pinnix, known affectionately around Kernersville as "Neighbor," was remembered by Reverend H.B. Johnson shortly after his death in 1963. The name Pinnix, for folks in Kernersville, conjures images of a drugstore, where people gathered to gossip and catch up on the latest news and a man, working behind the counter filling prescriptions, ready to greet his neighbors with a friendly "howdy, neighbor," thus earning him his nickname.

Born in 1882, Neighbor Pinnix was the son of Reverend J.W. Pinnix, a local schoolteacher, and his wife, Victoria Caffey Pinnix. At the age of eighteen, Neighbor found himself working for Dr. B.J. Sapp, who ran the hotel in town and used one room of the hotel as a pharmacy. Neighbor quickly discovered an interest in his work and began borrowing books from his boss. When he felt he was ready, Neighbor traveled to Raleigh, where he studied pharmacy and soon passed the North Carolina Pharmaceutical Board exam and obtained his license. He worked briefly in Raleigh, but as soon as he heard that a frame building was for sale on the crossroads in Kernersville, he made his way home, purchased the property and opened Pinnix Drug. The original Pinnix Drug was in an old frame house that sat on the corner of the crossroads. That was in 1904. Later, he would build the brick building we see today in that same location.

Interior of Pinnix Drug Store with J.M "Neighbor" Pinnix in 1914. *Courtesy Joe Pinnix.*

According to the 1940 census, Neighbor Pinnix reported that he worked seventy-five hours per week. From accounts of his life, he was probably underestimating the amount of time he spent working. According to his grandson, Joe Pinnix Jr., Neighbor never left Kernersville. He lived two doors down from the drugstore and walked to work, never owning a car: "My granddaddy never saw the ocean, never saw the mountains. He never went on vacation. He never wanted to leave Kernersville." Neighbor Pinnix worked hard to serve the community that he loved. He was in the drugstore by 7:00 a.m. and could often be found working from fourteen to eighteen hours a day. Often, he would go into the store in the middle of the night to fill prescriptions for sick friends and neighbors. Once, when Neighbor did go out of town to Winston-Salem to catch a Twins minor league baseball game, it made the front page of the *Kernersville News.*

During the 1930s, the Depression hit the United States hard, and the citizens of Kernersville felt the trying times just as much as the rest of the country. However, Kernersville had one saving grace. Neighbor Pinnix continued to work throughout the Depression, filling prescriptions as they came in. These prescriptions were filled, even if there was no money to pay the man who was filling them. Neighbor sacrificed his own credit to

Pinnix Drug, circa 1940. *Courtesy Joe Pinnix.*

ensure his neighbors did not go without any medication they needed. Even once the folks were able to go back to work, Neighbor never asked to be repaid. In a 1954 newspaper article, Neighbor is quoted as saying, "I've never asked them for it, don't intend to. But I still have their friendship. And that's more important."

Friends, neighbors and those who were teenagers and children during the 1940s to the 1960s have especially fond memories of Pinnix Drug. It was *the* place to get a cherry cola. (We have heard both Pepsi and Coke mentioned here, and we aren't brave enough to make a claim either way.) It was the place that many teenagers found their first jobs, working behind the soda fountain and fixing ice cream sundaes for their friends. Folks who were children in the 1950s and 1960s vividly recall visiting one of the local dentists who rented office space from Mr. Pinnix upstairs. After the "torture" they endured upstairs, they were quick to take their coins downstairs to treat themselves to candy and soda.

The space upstairs in the Pinnix Drug building was quite large. Various doctors and other businesses rented space upstairs. Some folks might be surprised to learn that there was also apartment space upstairs. For a while, Mr. Pinnix was renting the apartment space to State Bureau of Investigation (SBI) agents. We have no idea what state agents would be doing in Kernersville or why they needed space in a fairly sleepy little town like Kernersville. However, by the time this occurred, we know that Kernersville was a trucking hub for many companies, so there is speculation that they were investigating some of those companies.

Neighbor Pinnix went out of his way to accommodate his customers and kept up with the changing times. He had a telephone installed in the drugstore and allowed his customers to use it. When they began to use it more than he did, he had a second line installed in the pharmacy. He had a television in the drugstore in a time when most people did not have one in their homes, encouraging his customers to stay and enjoy it while he worked.

Although Neighbor was busy in the pharmacy, he found time to serve as an alderman for forty years. In 1921, when Neighbor was elected to his alderman seat, Kernersville was already beginning improvements to the town's quality of life. During his tenure, he helped usher in additional paved sidewalks, a municipal waterworks and a sewer system, ensuring that Kernersville was a desirable place to live. Neighbor Pinnix died on May 26, 1963, leaving a hole in the Kernersville community.

THE GHOST STORY

The Pinnix Drug building is an iconic piece of the Kernersville landscape. The drugstore, of course, took up the large main level. The second level of the building had many different uses. From dentists to SBI agents, the upstairs of the building seems to have had a life of its own. And now that the building is sitting empty, many folks have reported seeing movement in the upstairs windows. A park was recently constructed diagonally across from the old building, and it is a popular place. At any time of the day or evening, folks can be seen checking out the koi pond, enjoying the outdoor picnic tables and benches or meeting up with friends for a shopping trip. For the folks who like to "stop and smell the roses" and enjoy just watching the downtown daily comings and goings, many are now reporting seeing someone standing in the upstairs windows peering down at them. One gentleman reported that he had been sitting in the park enjoying a Mike & Mike's Italian Ice (try it if you get the chance) and clearly watched a man (or at least what he thought was a man) walk from one window to another, peaking through the blinds to look at the street. When the gentleman asked his companion if he saw it, his friend looked white as a sheet but shook his head no. When he pressed his friend, his companion angrily got up and left and now refuses to go back to the park. And that was in the middle of the day.

Another story that was reported to us recently could leave you with a warm and tingly feeling or an ice-cold feeling in your spine. Several friends had been enjoying themselves at Kernersville Brewing Company (see the Davis Hotel chapter). The group left the brewery and walked up Main Street. As the group went to cross Mountain to South Main Street, they noticed an older gentleman walking up the street toward the group. He was described as walking "purposely" toward the Pinnix Drug building. For whatever reason, the group found themselves mesmerized by the gentleman. He walked right up to the door, reached in his pocket and pulled out keys and began to unlock the door. Just then a fire truck siren pierced the night, and the group immediately looked toward the source of the noise. By the time they looked back, the gentleman was gone, and the building was empty and quiet. They debated what to do but ultimately came to the conclusion that since the man they saw was somewhat transparent, they really did not know who they could or should call. Some of the group chalk the experience up to enjoying too many refreshments at KBC, but others in the group insist it was real, since each person in the group saw exactly the same thing. One person in the group also swears that he heard the gentleman say, "Howdy, Neighbor."

THE FRANCIS MARION STAFFORD HOUSE

THE HISTORY

The Francis Marion Stafford House sits a little back from the south end of Main Street in Kernersville. The home marks the beginning of the historic district. It is a large, yellow frame home with a wraparound porch. It beckons guests and visitors to the front door with its warm and sunny exterior. As it is nestled in a grove of trees, you would never guess that the home backs up to Saint Paul's Cemetery, which dates to the early 1800s. The two places coexist peacefully and create a serene atmosphere. The Stafford House was originally a cabin built around 1840, and in 1856, Francis Stafford added a living room and bedroom above it. William Cornelius Stafford purchased the home from his father's estate in 1905 and continued to renovate and expand the home.

William Cornelius Stafford became a prominent citizen in Kernersville. He was a farmer, owned several different businesses, including briefly owning the local newspaper, and sold tobacco. He owned a popular mercantile that stayed in business long after he passed away, the W.C. Stafford store. Mr. Stafford was also the mayor of Kernersville from 1911 until 1913 and ushered in the first paved sidewalks in town while he was in office, helping to make Kernersville an even more attractive town to put down roots. He and his wife had five children.

Stafford-Greenfield House. *Kernersville Museum Foundation.*

The home located on the south end of Main Street stayed in the family, and in 1987, Sallie Greenfield, the great-granddaughter of Francis Marion Stafford, had the home moved from its original location at 635 South Main Street to where it sits today, a few hundred feet from its original location. Today, the home is still owned by Ms. Greenfield and operates as a bed-and-breakfast.

THE GHOST STORY

According to Sallie Greenfield, who is in her eighties, the Stafford House has been haunted for longer than she's been alive. And if moving the house down the street did not lose the ghost, it will probably remain haunted long after Ms. Greenfield is gone and able to apply for the job herself. More than likely, she will just want to meet this ghost she calls Annu and thank her for "keeping an eye" on her beloved family home for all these years since its earliest days.

The origin of the name Annu is somewhat mysterious. Was that the ghost's name or did someone name her? Ms. Greenfield can only say she is not sure if it is a Native American spirit or not. The name Annu has origins in multiple languages, so it is anyone's guess about where this spirit might have originated.

Oh, one more thing about Annu before this ghost story is told. Female visitors to the Stafford-Greenfield House who experience Annu's presence do not mind returning. However, males who have stayed there never want to go back. So, apparently, some issues stay with us even in the afterlife.

Now, let us examine the case of a female Moravian minister who was in town for a conference. Ms. Greenfield had opened the Stafford House to accommodate the visiting ministers. Two foreign female ministers were registered for the downstairs rooms, while our out-of-state minister would be staying upstairs.

After a long day of conferences, our minister from out of state made her way to the Stafford House and settled in for the night. After prayers and a fluff of the pillow, she recalled hearing her fellow ministers come into the house walking around, talking to each other and getting settled in for the evening. Knowing she would have an early flight, she could not afford to be social and visit. So, she got used to the noise and drifted off to sleep with plans to get up early the following morning and quietly leave the home so that she would not disturb those rowdy ministers below. She resisted temptation.

The next morning when she got up, she was surprised to hear they were already awake. She could hear them opening kitchen cabinets and rustling around the house. She got ready and planned to say hello to them when she left. At checkout, her surprise turned to amazement, or puzzlement, or possibly fear. What she found was an empty downstairs. Her inquiries were met with the disturbing fact that her housemates had never made it to the Stafford House. They ended up staying with some local parishioners they had dinner with the evening before. Annu is not the most conscientious of hosts, but at least she did not break anything this time.

Our Moravian minister gave the Stafford House a good rating. The next time the conference was held in the area, she called Ms. Greenfield and asked if she could stay in the Stafford House again and bring her daughter with her so that she too could experience the ghost of the Stafford House.

Although women seem to have an easy go of it at the Stafford House, as previously mentioned, it's the male visitors who do not fare as well. Ms. Greenfield recounted the story of a friend who was hosting a family reunion in Kernersville. Everyone attending found accommodations with family or friends in the area, except her son, whose schedule implied he would be there late that evening. Ms. Greenfield solved his problem by offering him a room at the Stafford House for the night. Although we are not sure exactly what happened in the house during the morning hours, we do know that the son left the Stafford House in the middle of the night and showed up at his parents' home, insisting that he would sleep on the couch if he had to, but he could not stay in that house all night long. Commitment issues. How did Annu know?

Another time, a gentleman was staying in the Stafford House with his service dog. The dog had always been a model of excellent behavior as a service animal, but one night in the Stafford House had the gentleman saying he would never stay there again. His dog had cried and whined all night long. He would cower behind his owner, refusing to do the simplest of tasks until the two left the home. It is understandable because the service dog was male. However, he had been fixed, so the mystery continues.

As for Sallie Greenfield herself, she feels comfortable in her family home and says that Annu is part of the home or family or staff, depending on your definition.

STUART MOTOR COMPANY

THE HISTORY

The building that currently sits at 109 East Mountain Street in downtown Kernersville was built by Ned Stuart in 1924. The spot was an ideal location for the new and booming automobile repair business. J.R. Stuart & Son had been in business in Kernersville since 1920. Ned and his father, J.R. Stuart, had previously operated their business out of a location on Bodenhamer Street. J.R. had forty-two years of machine shop experience, working in Winston-Salem before moving to Kernersville. J.R.'s son, Ned, had specialized in auto repair, gaining experience in Knoxville, Tennessee; Richmond, Virginia; and Asheville before joining his father in his garage in Kernersville. By 1920, J.R. and Ned had expanded their interests and became dealers in hardware, farm machinery and automobile supplies while operating a modern garage.

By 1924, Ned Stuart had purchased land on East Mountain Street, next to where the old inn at the crossroads had sat, and began work to build a new garage. J.R. Stuart remained open as a hardware store, while Ned's business was focused on automobile work. The new, two-story building was brick and designed with an eye toward future endeavors, with large windows facing East Mountain Street. Ned had recently organized the Town of Kernersville's first fire department. Before this, everyone in town responded to fires, but with only a bucket brigade and volunteers

Stuart Motor Company. *Photo by author.*

pulling water from wells, fires had routinely ravaged homes and businesses in Kernersville. In 1923, Ned organized the Kernersville Volunteer Fire Department, and the town purchased a 1923 La France fire truck for $6,500. Today, you can see this same truck sitting inside the new Ladder 42 Fire Station on Highway 66 in Kernersville. Ned Stuart would serve as the town's first fire chief for many years, and he organized the volunteers and their training while housing the new fire truck in his garage until a station was completed in 1928.

By 1927, the Stuarts had opened Kernersville's first automobile showroom. By 1930, the Stuart Motor Company was the city's first Ford Dealership. Ned, continuing to expand his business, soon purchased a Model T tow truck and added towing and recovery to the list of services he offered. The Stuart Motor Company remained in business until 1986. After this, the building was repurposed. The front of the building was converted into office space, while the garage portion remained unused until 2004, when a local attorney purchased the building and converted the space into his law office.

The Stuart Motor Company has a historical marker dedicated to the building. The marker reads:

Stuart Motor Company Est. 1926 by Ned R. & Annabel Stuart

The building was originally opened as Kernersville's First Auto Showroom and is on the National Register of Historic Places.

Due to the many hats Ned Stuart wore while serving the town it was used as: The First Hudson Essex & Ford Dealer, Office of the Fire Chief, Police Commission, Town Commissioner, Head of the School Board, Town Building Inspector, and Civil Defense Warden in WWII.

The building served as a town meeting place for many civic groups in the early years. The apartments above not only housed the Stuart Family, Ned, Annabel, sons Ned Jr., & Robert, but served as the first homes for many of the towns founding Fathers.

Restored in 1986 by Ned Jr., wife June & son Bryan.

The building was listed on the National Register of Historic Places in 1988.

THE GHOST STORY

A ghostly stereotype is that of the haunted house. It does not always have to be a house. And usually, the ghosts are just floating aimlessly around the kitchen or the hallways. They could have a purpose when they float. They could be at work. Consider Stuart Motor Company. Late at night, the current tenants sometimes hear muffled voices in the next room when that room is empty, but it's the folks walking down the sidewalk, at an hour when they should be home, who hear and see so much more.

Garage doors can be heard opening and closing around the Stuart Building. The clinging sound of tools being dropped on a cement floor and bouncing to a stop is a common report by these late-night strollers. One secondhand night walker's story goes as follows.

A young man was out and about in downtown Kernersville one late evening when he noticed the lights were on at a local business. It was not the restaurant or brewery, and looking in the window, he could see mechanics hard at work repairing cars and trucks. Many of you are probably thinking, "Out and about in downtown Kernersville one late evening. This guy is in desperate need of a social life." Well, you might be missing the point of this story. The point is, he was seeing the Stuart Motor Company as it was years ago. It was a ghostly vision of a time gone by—not when mechanics worked late hours. It was a sight of a spectral nature. He was seeing a ghost, a fellow human being now passed, but one clinging to an earthly way of life.

He stood and watched them for a while. It was curious. It was nostalgic. It was wrong. This place had not been a garage for years. He looked away, closed his eyes and shook his head. The reset worked. He now saw the dark silhouette of the Stuart Building that contained only law offices. He could not explain it, but he knew what he saw was real. The faint smell of gas and oil lingering in the air and the sound of a wrench being thrown back in a toolbox as he walked away just confirmed his vision.

What are we to make of this? Most ghost stories are of the personal encounter variety. This one was an ethereal pageant of yesteryear. In the paranormal world, this was a privilege and nothing that would make one scared. In the normal world, the fact that mechanics can charge for labor throughout eternity is frightening.

The Academy

The History

Education would prove to be an important part of Kernersville's history. According to Michael Marshall and Jerry Taylor, in their book, *Kernersville: The First 125 Years*, a small private school was erected in 1840 by Joseph Kerner's sons, John F. and Phillip Kerner, for their children. By 1855, well before Kernersville was even recognized as a town, a female academy had been established by William P. Henley, who had acquired the inn at the Crossroads that had been owned by Joseph Kerner. The school likely stayed in operation for a few years, but by 1857, a coeducational school was erected and named the Kernersville Academy. These schools were not like the public schools we know today, and students had to pay a tuition and fees to attend. The building that was built to house this school was originally located where S&R Motor Company stands today, and a marker is located there for those interested in seeing it.

It is interesting to note that while many schools were closing during the Civil War, the Kernersville Academy continued to operate, according to Marshall and Taylor. It was not until 1905 that the State of North Carolina passed a law that created a free public school in Kernersville. The Kernersville Academy remained in operation until the free public school was opened. Due to a fire, the new public school even operated briefly out of the old Kernersville Academy building. Trustees for the school purchased two acres of land on East Mountain Street near where town

Kernersville Academy, 1909. *North Carolina State Archives.*

hall and the Kernersville Chamber of Commerce sit today. In 1906, the new public school building was completed. It was built in brick with arched windows marking the front of the building. The structure featured a cupola that housed a bell that was previously used by the Kernersville Academy.

The building operated for almost twenty years. Sadly, on the last day of 1925, during the Christmas recess, the handsome building caught fire. To this day, it is a mystery how the building would have caught fire, since school was not in session, and no one was inside the building. Once the fire was put out, citizens were surely sad to see that there was no way to use what remained of the building. This forced all 550 students to be sent to neighboring schools. According to Marshall and Taylor, citizens at the time of the fire speculated on the cause of the fire, with some believing that it was started on purposes and believing they knew who might have started it. However, those names and motives have been lost to time.

The town would eventually recover from the fire, and a new school was completed in 1927 on land purchased on West Mountain Street, where Kernersville Elementary sits today.

THE GHOST STORY

The Kernersville Chamber of Commerce, located at 136 East Mountain Street, is where local businesses meet to network, fundraise and learn more about the community. But its membership is not the only thing that the staff thinks visits them. Employees of the chamber have felt cool presences in the hallways after hours. With almost no windows on the left side of the building, shadows creep around at night and have staff puzzle over inanimate objects for far too long trying to figure out what is staring at them.

Lights have been known to come on by themselves, often after they've been turned off in no longer occupied offices, turning on in the middle of the night to greet them when they come in the next morning or flickering off in meetings. Maintenance workers have checked the wiring, and there are no issues that can be found. The staff often hears unrecognized voices drifting through the hallways, seemingly with no origin. Occasionally, it is the giggle of children that unnerves the staff. Office items, like a computer mouse, will often disappear along with other keepsakes, only to reappear later at another location. Oftentimes, a slight knock can be heard randomly throughout the hallways, leading the staff to believe they have a visitor. When they go to investigate, no one is there, but there is a creepy feeling that someone was just there and is playing a trick on them.

Could it be the energy of the children who missed out on finishing up their educational experience due to the fire? We will probably never know. But we do know that the staff refuses to spend too much time alone in the building, preferring to leave together in the evenings if they have had a late event.

Dunlap Springs

The History

If you know anything about very old folk music, you may know the name Naomi Wise, or at least "Poor Naomi" or even "Omi Wise." Doc Watson, legendary North Carolinian who practically invented playing Appalachian folk music on a flattop guitar, popularized Naomi's story when he released "Omi Wise" in May 1964.

Naomi's story was so tragic and disturbing that it still haunts those who know it more than two hundred years later. Naomi, who was born in 1789, was said to be a beautiful young woman. She was an orphan who was raised in the home of William Adams in the New Salem community in Randolph County. Across the border in Guilford County lived a young man named Jonathan Lewis, who took a job working for a man in Asheboro. His route to work took him by the Adams cabin, where he met and fell in love with Naomi Wise. But an orphan was not what Jonathan's mother had in mind for her son. She encouraged her son to court the wife of the man who employed him.

Soon, rumors persisted that Naomi was in the family way and Jonathan was said to be the father. Publicly, Jonathan dismissed the rumors. Privately, he professed his love for Naomi. We will never know what exactly happened the night Naomi snuck out of her home to meet Jonathan. Surely, she thought she was running toward a happy future. But Jonathan had different plans. In 1808, Naomi's body was found in the Deep River, floating face down, and Jonathan stood trial for her murder. Apparently, Jonathan even uttered a confession to the grisly deed on his deathbed.

None of this happened in Kernersville. But what *is* in Kernersville is the spring that was the original fountainhead of the Deep River. So, when the mineral springs craze swept the United States, the owners of the property where the spring was located looked around and realized that they might have a great source of income on their hands. Naming the springs Naomi Springs after the still popular, if utterly tragic, figure of Naomi Wise was probably a great way to grab the attention of potential customers. But what to sell? Bottled water, of course, at least in the beginning. As early as April 1912, we began to see Naomi Springs, as well as Naomi Heights, show up in newspaper articles. Described as sitting one mile east of Kernersville (that is, one mile east of the crossroads), the springs were reported as beginning to be developed by a corporation that had plans to add a hotel to the property. The owner of the springs, J.A. Stone, sent a sample of the water off to a "well-known" chemist in Virginia to have the water analyzed. Already, the property contained a small farm and building lots. By June of that same year, the analysis had come back, and reports boasted, "The Finest Mineral Water on Earth Here at Home" and the "Famous Naomi Spring Water." Later that same month, Mr. Stone announced plans for not just a hotel but also a summer resort on the property. And by July, the Ladies' Aid Society had begun to host lawn parties on the property. One report from July 30, 1912, in the *Winston-Salem Journal* reported, "Our citizens are terribly interested and well pleased with the Naomi Mineral Spring water. They visit the spring early and late often going down as early as the first dawn of day and by moonlight in the evening. It is becoming quite a resort for picnickers and other gatherings for amusement. To add to the pleasure of the resort the Kernersville Brass Band occasionally goes down and enlivens the occasion with music. The analysis of the water shows a high percent of mineral and it is proving to be of medicinal properties."

By August, a lake was being constructed on the property. Much was quiet over the winter, but in the spring of 1913, reports began rolling in about the Naomi Mineral Springs Water Co. and the shipping of mineral water to all parts of the state. A modern bottling plant was being installed, and the roads were being improved so that they could ship their product more effectively. By early that summer, advertisements began to appear detailing the chemical analysis of the water, with the chemist who performed the tests attesting to the helpfulness of the water in treating "many chronic affections of the digestive system from catarrhal condition of the stomach; rheumatism, gout and other kidney troubles," to name a few. The advertisements end with the promise of thoroughly sterilized shipping carboys.

After this, each year, the local newspapers were frequently detailing the trips and social outings that were taking place at Naomi Springs. Surely, this was a place the locals were proud of, right here in their own town. The development of the land with a hotel resort that could be open year-round was a hot topic during the summer of 1915. Finally, by September 1915, it was announced in the local papers that Naomi Springs and the sixty-four acres that surrounded it had been sold to a Mr. J.H. Dunlap of Bonlee in Chathama County. Mr. Dunlap did indeed plan to build a hotel and develop the property into a summer and winter resort. The land was sold for $7,500, roughly the equivalent of $200,000 in 2020.

In 1916, an article in the *Twin-City Sentinel* described the scene at Naomi Springs, stating that it had become an "exceedingly popular resort for picnickers." Every afternoon and evening finds large crowds of visitors there drinking the mineral water and enjoying their picnic suppers. "On Thursday afternoon of this week a party came up from Oak Ridge about six o'clock. An hour was spent in playing rook and other games on the knoll overlooking the Springs. Then supper was spread, being thoroughly enjoyed by all present. The ride home was made about 9:30 o'clock in the moonlight"

Spring House at Dunlap Springs postcard. *Durwood Barbour Collection of North Carolina postcards, UNC–Chapel Hill archives.*

It certainly sounds like an ideal place to enjoy an afternoon. Schools, church groups, social clubs and even large groups of friends frequently made their way to the mineral springs to partake in the waters and enjoy their surroundings. By 1917, the name had officially been changed to Dunlap Springs and a large pavilion had been built on the knoll that overlooked the springs. Often Japanese lanterns were hung in the new pavilion and musical bands performed for the groups that gathered. However, as plans were being made to finally build the hotel on the property, America entered World War I, and those plans were put on hold temporarily. Mr. Dunlap allowed the locals to come and enjoy his property and only charged them a fee when they took the mineral water in large quantities.

By 1920, the hotel was finally complete and opened for guests on July 19. A formal dance was held to celebrate the occasion. Part of the hotel was reserved for traveling men and wives. The handsome brick hotel and rooms were described as "light and airy" with weekly rates ranging anywhere from fifteen to eighteen dollars; daily rates were three dollars, lodging was one dollar and a single meal was seventy-five cents. The hotel contained forty rooms, a lobby and a dining room that had a seating capacity for one hundred guests.

Dunlap Springs enjoyed popularity and prosperity for the next several years. But all good things must come to an end. As the seeds of unrest

Dunlap Springs Hotel as pictured in a postcard, 1925. *Durwood Barbour Collection of North Carolina postcards, UNC–Chapel Hill archives.*

Lobby of Dunlap Springs Hotel as pictured in a postcard, 1925. *Durwood Barbour Collection of North Carolina postcards, UNC–Chapel Hill archives.*

began to grow in the United States at the end of the 1920s, the Dunlap family surely felt the squeeze. In 1927, the family mortgaged the property. By 1929, when the Great Depression was in full swing, the hotel was closed. The property sold at a public auction in 1931. At this point, trustees at Bethel Bible College purchased the property and began operating a school out of the hotel. A strict code of conduct, as well as the need to charge tuition during a time when money was scarce for most folks during the Great Depression, caused the school to close its doors by 1933. However, local authors Mike Marshall and Jerry Taylor found that the government pressed the hotel into use in 1934. The Emergency Relief Administration (ERA), one of Franklin Roosevelt's famous "alphabet agencies," used the hotel to provide quarters for "old and infirm men." According to their research, the men "who were able to work repaired and reconditioned the buildings, cleaned the grounds, consisting of 60 acres, planted shrubbery and trimmed trees." The report Marshall and Taylor referenced also noted that "the spring at this camp has proved a great help to these older men. Their general health has improved and at this time there has been no illness of a serious nation." The government used the property until March 1936.

By 1940, what was once Dunlap Springs was purchased by a couple from Greensboro, North Carolina, and deeded to the Southern District of the

Dining room of Dunlap Springs as pictured in a postcard, 1925. *Durwood Barbour Collection of North Carolina postcards, UNC–Chapel Hill archives.*

Pilgrim Holiness Church for the purposes of creating a church college and high school. After repairs, the school was opened in 1946.

The next thirty-five years would see the addition of more buildings and the changing of the name of the school from the Southern Pilgrim Bible College to Kernersville Wesleyan College. By 1971, the college stopped operating, but the high school continued on until 1981, when it moved to merge with Wesleyan Christian Academy in High Point, North Carolina. In 1984, Joe Dudley and his wife, Eunice, purchased the property and operated Dudley Cosmetology University until around 2008.

The spring itself eventually ran dry, and sadly, the construction of the business section of Interstate 40, now known as Salem Parkway, ran over where the spring once brought so much joy to so many people. The old campus can still be seen, although now it sits empty. The original building was torn down at some point. A newer hotel was built close to where the original one would have been located, and it was built in a style reminiscent of the old hotel. It, too, sits empty today, waiting for someone to come along and see its potential and breathe fresh life into the property.

The Ghost Story

One thing we hope you have noticed with our tales of the afterlife is that the ghosts that roam in Kernersville are not scary or malicious. They seem to seek to do no harm. Some of them are here to look after the properties they find themselves attached to. Some of them are just passing through, while some of them tend to be a bit mischievous. Traditionally, ghosts are thought to be someone who departed life quickly, leaving unfinished business to attend to—maybe someone who has messages left to give others. Often their fates are tied to tragic incidents that caused them to take their lives. However, much like Kernersville itself is unique, the ghosts here are unique too.

Take the ghosts that are said to be at the old Dunlap Springs property. People have often reported hearing brass band music coming from the woods. Teenagers who either attended the schools that were on the property later, or ones who found themselves exploring the property of their own accord, have reported trying to follow the music—hearing it get louder, thinking they were getting closer, only for the music to fade and the teens to find themselves walking in circles in the wooded property. Some often hear women laughing, as though they are having a great time, but they are never actually found.

Across the main road from the property are several residential homes. A gentleman recently came into the museum and recounted this tale for the staff. As a teenager, his family lived in a home near where the Bible College was located (Dunlap Springs). He and his then girlfriend where driving around one evening looking for something to do. They decided that even though it was getting dark, they thought it would be fun to sneak onto the property of the college and see what was going on. So off they went, hand in hand, trying to creep onto the property without being seen. As they crossed onto the campus, the couple heard music and saw the glow of lights. The gentleman, let's call him Tim, told his girlfriend that it must be a party. He told her that they could probably walk right up to the rest of the partygoers and join in and no one would even notice that they didn't actually belong there. Tim's girlfriend reluctantly agreed with his plan because she heard the music and saw the faint glow of lights. The two headed off toward the sounds of the party, only to find that there was nothing there. Tim was sure that if they just reached the top of a small hill, they would find the source of the music, but once they crested the hill, they were met with nothing but a quiet wooded area. At this point, Tim said his girlfriend got the heebie-jeebies and wanted to go home. Tim agreed and told her they must have imagined the music and faint lights. The couple turned and started making their way off the property. Once they were about halfway back to where they crossed onto the property, Tim's girlfriend stopped abruptly. "Do you hear that?" she whispered. Tim stopped. It was the music again. Tim was almost afraid to look over his shoulder; he didn't know why he was afraid— he just was. When he finally looked, he saw the faint glow of lights again, just over the hill they had walked away from. Scratching his head in confusion, he looked at his girlfriend. Her face was a little pale, but she shrugged her shoulders and offered, "Maybe we are not invited."

Tim said they went on back to his house and never told anyone else what had happened. When the staff at the museum asked him what he thought it was, Tim grinned and said, "I think they were having a party and my girlfriend was right, we weren't invited, so we couldn't see it." Tim explained that he was creeped out by the experience but was more intrigued than anything.

So, maybe the ghosts that haunt Kernersville are just interested in having a good time. The town that has always been known for its hospitality might just be too good to leave. Maybe those who came before us aren't quite ready to let go of this town, or maybe they are watching to make sure we take care of it. In any case, we hope our tales haven't made you less inclined to come and explore our little part of North Carolina. Who knows, once you come for a visit, you may never want to leave either.

PART II

THE WATER TOWER

ONE LAST TALE, BUT THIS ONE HAS NO GHOSTS

It seems odd to end a book about ghost stories in our town with a tale that has no ghosts. We have included this tale because it is one that gets discussed to this day, and we hope these men will be remembered. It was a tragedy for this small town to bear witness to, and it would seem that in its unfolding, more than just the memory of the day's events would be left. But thankfully, the spirts are at rest in this section of town, and for that, we are grateful.

September 25, 1984, dawned a warm and sunny day. It was, I am sure, one of those days when folks were just itching for cooler weather, wondering when fall would make its appearance. I would love to tell you that it is uncommon here, in this part of the South, to experience days when the temperature reaches eighty-seven degrees and the humidity hits you at more than 70 percent throughout the day that late in September, but this book is clearly listed as nonfiction, and the story I am about to tell you is, sadly, very much true.

Charles Tompkins was nineteen years old and had been on his job with the Westbrook Iron Company in Lumberton, North Carolina, for just four short months. When a job came up in Kernersville, North Carolina, Brenda Tompkins, eighteen, decided to come to work with her husband. She did not like being away from him for too long. By that Tuesday, Brenda and Charles had been in Kernersville for several days as Charles and other members

Water tower that was located in downtown Kernersville, 1940. *Kernersville Museum Foundation.*

of his crew had worked to tear down the old water tower that sat right in the middle of downtown Kernersville, just behind the main square. The town had opted to stop using the old tower and had hired Westbrook Iron Company to come in and carefully dismantle the pieces of the tower.

According to the *Sentinel*, Brenda Tompkins, had stated, "We have been married such a short time that we are still considered honeymooners," and "I felt better being near him and something just told me to come this time. I didn't think the Kernersville job would take long."

The young woman had sat in the alley during the day and watched her young husband work, carefully cutting away pieces of what was left of the old water tower. At the end of the day, Charles made one last cut. The inexperienced worker must have miscalculated the angle of the cut because the beam came back at Charles and pinned him to another beam, breaking both of his legs. Rescue workers were at the scene almost immediately, while Brenda watched from the ground as attempts were made to save her husband. Initially, workers felt confident that they would be able to free Charles and get him to a hospital. Brenda too felt confident in the beginning, telling a small group of people who were keeping vigil with her, "medically, he must be in good shape, and now all they have to do is get near him."

The first rescuer to the scene was a man named Dale Roberts. He quickly climbed the water tower's leg in his tennis shoes and no safety belt to assess the damage to the victim. He climbed down to grab the medical supplies he needed and get a safety harness on. Another rescue worker arrived, and together, they were quick to stop the external bleeding that they could find. Between the two rescue workers, the men were able to free one of Charles's legs, but they could not manage to free him totally, and one leg remained trapped. Roberts worked on Charles for two hours before he climbed down and promptly blacked out from exhaustion. He was taken to a local hospital, but Charles was still not freed.

From the ground, a 75-foot aerial unit from nearby Winston-Salem was dispatched to the scene, but it was of no help since Charles was at least 119 feet off the ground. Next, a cherry picker (which is a type of crane) was dispatched to the scene, but it was only 90 feet tall.

In a final attempt to rescue Charles, a helicopter was sent from nearby Winston-Salem. By the time the helicopter took off, Charles had taken his last breath. Rescuers who had been with Charles throughout the evening reported that Charles was calm throughout the ordeal, although he was in tremendous pain. He asked his rescuers to not leave him. The last thing he said was that he did not want to die. Once it became clear that Charles had passed, Brenda was moved away from the scene and told of her husband's fate. Town officials arranged to get Brenda to her closest family members. As they had her in the car, the helicopter was approaching the scene in an attempt to free her husband's body.

The rescue workers communicated with the helicopter pilot that there was no longer a need to rush to the scene, that the mission was now body removal. The helicopter pilot, a man named Thomas Haroski, and a rescue worker named Steve Richey, chose to continue their mission. While dipping the helicopter lower to the scene on their arrival, something went terribly wrong. The water tower that Charles was dismantling was located just a few hundred feet from several buildings. It was late in the evening by the time the helicopter got to the scene, a little after 10:00 p.m. The men dropped a seventy-five-foot rope out of the helicopter, hoping to be able to tie the rope around Charles and lift his body away from the terrible scene. When the rope failed to reach the body, the helicopter decided to dip lower. Crews on the ground were radioing the pilot to make sure he understood that the mission had moved from a rescue situation to a body recovery. At the time, workers on the ground were not sure if Haroski heard their message but later were told that in fact the pilot did understand the situation. It is not clear if Haroski did not see the pole that he was dangerously close to, but somehow, the blade of the helicopter clipped a remaining leg of the water tower, causing the helicopter to hit yet another leg that had yet to be removed. The helicopter turned end over end, catching fire and landing on top of a nearby apartment building. Haroski and his passenger, Richey, were both killed in the crash.

And as if the day was not already terrible enough, the crash caused a gas main to erupt and leak until the following morning. According to several newspaper reports, at least 350 people were standing on the ground watching these horrific scenes unfold in the center of downtown Kernersville. At the time, the entire population of Kernersville was around 10,000.

On talking with Charles Tompkins's family, it was discovered that the teenager was making just $4.00 per hour (minimum wage at this time was only $3.10). The young couple had only $18.00 between the two of them. In true Kernersville fashion, by the day after the horrific accident, an account had been opened in Brenda Tompkins's name, and the citizens of Kernersville came together and raised several hundred dollars to help the young widow out.

News of the day's tragic events reached all over the United States. Newspapers in California, New York, Vermont, Mississippi and Ohio ran the story of the rescue helicopter that crashed, killing the two rescue workers as they attempted to recover the body of a young man who had bled to death in front of an entire town.

Later that evening, in a cruel twist of fate, rescue workers learned of the availability of a crane that they would use to remove the body of Charles Tompkins. Had they known about it earlier in the day, Tompkins might have survived, and the helicopter never would have been dispatched.

There is no ghost story that goes along with this terribly sad tale. I have spent many evenings on the block across from where this accident took place and have personally never seen or heard anything that made me think it was haunted. Possibly because the people who died in this accident did not live in Kernersville, so they are not connected to this place. But this incident has definitely made its mark on this small town. Almost everyone I meet can tell me where they were when this happened, if they stood in the street or if they were made to go home by their parents who did not want them to see what was happening. A local attorney told me that his dad was called to the scene because he worked for the local power company and they thought maybe he could offer some assistance. Not knowing what had happened, his dad asked if he wanted to come along. Being around seven years old at the time, he jumped at the chance to go anywhere with his dad. Once they arrived on the scene, his dad made him sit in the truck for several hours, not wanting him to see what was happening just beyond the truck. He recounted that he stared at the side of the building for what felt like hours sitting in that truck. To this day, when he sees the side of that building, the memory of that night will come flooding back.

It was a traumatic event for everyone in town and one that was heard throughout the United States. Newspapers from across the country reported on the story of the rescue helicopter that crashed trying to retrieve the body of a young man in the middle of downtown Kernersville.

CONCLUSION

We truly hope that you have enjoyed the history and the hauntings of our little town. Kernersville grew right in the heart of the Triad, and its people grew right along with it. We hope that we have conveyed the spirt of welcomeness that is inherently a part of this place. Kernersville has a long history of opening its arms to newcomers and making them feel like they have been here all along. We rarely meet a stranger, and if we do, we are quick to put them at ease. So please do not let our spooky tales put you off from visiting us. You will find the folks here just as warm and welcoming as ever. And as you have read, many of the folks who live here have loved Kernersville so much that they just never want to leave.

BIBLIOGRAPHY

Books and Periodicals

Curtis, Wayne. *And a Bottle of Rum, Revised and Updated: A History of the New World in Ten Cocktails*. New York: Broadway Books, 2018.

Fries, Adelaide L. *Forsyth County*. Salem, NC: Nabu Press, 1898.

———. *The Road to Salem*. Chapel Hill: University of North Carolina Press, 1944.

Fries, Adelaide, Stuart Thurman Wright and J. Edwin Hendrick. *Forsyth: The History of a County on the March*. Chapel Hill: University of North Carolina Press, 1976.

Hobbs, S. Huntington, Jr. *North Carolina: An Economic and Social Profile*. Chapel Hill: University of North Carolina Press, 1958.

Körner, Jules Gilmer, Jr. *Joseph of Kernersville*. Durham, NC: Seeman Printery, 1958.

Marshall, Michael, and Jerry Taylor. *Kernersville: The First 125 Years, 1778–1903*. Dallas: Primedia E-launch, 2015.

———. *Remembering Kernersville*. Charleston, SC: The History Press, 2010.

———. *Wicked Kernersville: Rogues, Robbers, Ruffians, & Rumrunners*. Charleston, SC: The History Press, 2009.

Owens, Eugene D. *Bethel Bible College Bulletin*, no. 1 (1932). UNC Chapel Hill Libraries.

Selected Online Sources

1860–1940 United States Census, Forsyth County, North Carolina. *Ancestry.com.*

Forsyth County, North Carolina (website). "Detailed Property Information Online Records." http://tellus.co.forsyth.nc.us/lrcpwa.

———. "Register of Deeds Online Records System." http://www.forsythdeeds.com/disclaimer.php.

Guilford County, North Carolina (website). "Register of Deeds Online Records System." http://rdlxweb.guilfordcountync.gov.

North Carolina Land Grants. http://www.nclandgrants.com.

Stokes County, North Carolina (website). "Register of Deeds Online Records System." http://www.co.stokes.nc.us/deeds.

Surry County, North Carolina (website). "Register of Deeds Online Records System." https://www.co.surry.nc.us/departments/(k_through_z)/register_of_deeds/record_search.php.

Selected Newspapers (Accessed via Newspapers.com)

Asheville-Citizen Times
Charlotte Observer
Greensboro Daily Record
Greensboro Patriot
Greensboro Record
High Point Enterprise
Kernersville News
Winston-Salem Journal
Winston-Salem Journal and Sentinel
(Winston-Salem) People's Press
(Winston-Salem) Twin-City Sentinel
(Winston-Salem) Union Republican
(Winston-Salem) Western Sentinel

Postcards

"Dunlaps Mineral Springs, Kernersville, North Carolina." Durwood Barbour Collection of North Carolina Postcards (P077), North Carolina Collection Photographic Archives, Wilson Library, UNC–Chapel Hill.

"Main Street, Looking North, Kernserville, N.C." Durwood Barbour Collection of North Carolina Postcards (P077), North Carolina Collection Photographic Archives, Wilson Library, UNC–Chapel Hill.

"Main Street, South, Kernersville, N.C." Durwood Barbour Collection of North Carolina Postcards (P077), North Carolina Collection Photographic Archives, Wilson Library, UNC–Chapel Hill.

"Southern Railway Station, Kernersville, N.C." Durwood Barbour Collection of North Carolina Postcards (P077), North Carolina Collection Photographic Archives, Wilson Library, UNC–Chapel Hill.

ABOUT THE AUTHORS

Kelly McGuire Hargett was born and raised in western North Carolina in the foothills of the Blue Ridge Mountains. She graduated from the University of North Carolina at Charlotte in 2001 with degrees in both history and communication studies. She went on to receive a master's degree in education from Western Carolina University and a post bac certificate in history from the University of Nebraska at Kearney. She worked in the North Carolina Community College system for many years and taught several history classes as an adjunct instructor in North Carolina, Kansas and Ohio. She has a great love for local history. She currently works as the executive director of the Kernersville Museum, where she truly enjoys hearing the local history from the people of Kernersville and preserving it for the next generation. She lives in Kernersville, North Carolina, with her husband, Jason; her two daughters, Laney and Kayson; two overly large dogs named Blue and Sheba; and one insane house cat that rules the roost named Goose.

Scott Icenhower retired to Kernersville from the world of finance with his wife, Katie Jo. They share a passion for all things theater and are now able to pursue their dream full time. Scott is a published playwright and author and is working to build a performance venue with his wife in downtown Kernersville. The couple plan to haunt the theater after they're gone. So, perhaps in a much later edition of this book you can catch up with these two again.